Lenin's Grandchildren

PRESCHOOL EDUCATION IN THE SOVIET UNION

BY

Kitty D. Weaver

WITH PHOTOGRAPHS BY HENRY WEAVER

SIMON AND SCHUSTER · NEW YORK

SBN 671-20798-9
LIBRARY OF CONGRESS CATALOG CARD NUMBER: 79-133096
DESIGNED BY EVE METZ
MANUFACTURED IN THE UNITED STATES OF AMERICA
BY THE BOOK PRESS, NEW YORK

FOR PEOPLE WHO LIKE CHILDREN

·CONTENTS·

·INTRODUCTION·

BY FRED M. HECHINGER

THE SOVIET UNION, not unlike the United States, is intensely child-oriented. Russian parents, and particularly grandmothers, tend to be protective of small children in a way that can be quite literally embarrassing to American visitors. It is not at all unusual for an American mother to be subjected to a public lecture from alarmed and indignant elderly Russian women in a public park if she allows her small child to stray a few hundred yards. To Russians, this is a sign of neglect and deserves at least a mild, grandmotherly tongue-lashing.

The slightest breeze, on an early-spring day, causes Russian babies to be bundled up so tightly that my more hardy Western spirits went out to these coddled tots in sympathy. On the other side of the coin, when I proudly showed snapshots of our two boys, then six and barely two years old, and both of them (I thought) the picture of health, the very competent lady in charge of a very well-run Moscow nursery school smiled and said, "Why don't you send us your babies so we can fatten them up?" Having just sampled the day's heavy lunch, I knew just what she meant.

The foreign visitor cannot help being amazed to find, amid the drab fashions on the streets and the generally sparse and unimaginative displays in Soviet shops, that little children in nursery schools and kindergarten are dressed in gay, colorful, and fashionable attire. In striking contrast to other consumer goods, children's toys, well made and full of fun, are for sale in acres of special stores.

It is probably true, as students of Soviet society suggest, that an economic ideology that discourages (and until fairly recently forbade) any accumulation of personal property tends to heap its riches on the children. Not unlike many Americans, moreover, today's Soviet parents want to give their children what they themselves were not allowed to cry for as infants, and the psychological drive in that direction is undoubtedly more compelling in a country that says you can't take it with you.

But while there are important similarities between American and Russian attitudes toward children, there is an important difference: the Soviets have long been devoting educational and institutional energies to a field we are only just in the process of discovering—preschool education.

It is fair and somewhat ironic to say that the Soviet approach to preschool child care and education is predominantly pragmatic, while the traditional American opposition to it has been largely ideological. In the old-fashioned American view, children (like women) belonged in, and to, the home. The Russian approach (which incidentally is not too different from the Scandinavian and Israeli practice) tended to be shrugged off as a political, totalitarian effort to take little tots away from their parents and indoctrinate them. In fact, of course, every society indoctrinates its children. This process takes place in American homes as well as in Soviet nursery schools. And, it must be added, the human tendency to think of children as "abandoned" to the school is not unknown to Russians. The director of a Moscow nursery school told me that she periodically calls her parents together to scold them for bringing their children toys and candy every evening at pick-up time. "I know they're doing this not so much because they love their children as because they feel guilty for having left them with us all day," she said.

The real issue, of course, is not whether it would be better if the things offered to preschoolers in nursery school could be done for them at home. The fact is that few, if any, homes can provide the opportunities of professional care *in the company of other children.* Indeed, the Soviet preschool approach can teach American parents and teachers a good deal about effective ways to make children take their place as constructive members in a group.

It will be said that the Soviets deliberately introduce such behavior because it is important preparation for the key demand on the Communist man—submission to the state. Undoubtedly there is some truth to this, since it is quite obvious that the Soviet school prepares children for life in the Communist state, just as the American school tries to condition children for life in the American type of representative democracy. But the point that is often missed is that excessive stress on the individual is as potentially dangerous as excessive domination by the group: neither egocentricity nor the suppression of the self is the answer. There is room for some crossbreeding of American and Russian pedagogy.

Most of all, there is room for an objective and open-minded study of the Soviet preschool experience, not to imitate it blindly but to extract from it those aspects of child care and teaching which can be adapted to the American need. This is particularly true at a time when preschool education is—far too late—at last swimming into public focus. With the relatively recent introduction of Head Start, insistent new demands for day-care centers for working mothers, and the Nixon Administration's avowed interest in new programs to deal with the children's years from two to five, the country appears ready for a break with the tradition that has pretended that all children—rich and poor alike—were getting their intellectual, psychological, social, and physical preschool education and care at home.

A great deal of trial and error can be avoided if the experience and lessons of other nations are at last given an intelligent hearing, without fear of ideological contamination. There is much in education, as in science, that is immune to ideological differences, or rather outside and above them. At any rate, the politics of educational practice can readily be distilled out of any approach

before it is transplanted to a different society with its own ide-
ologies. Quite apart from the politics of the state, children and
their basic needs are remarkably alike everywhere.

This is why Kitty Weaver's book constitutes a particularly
timely service. It properly stresses what Russian preschool education does rather than what its theorists claim it does. It enters
the classroom, observes the games, and lets children and teachers
speak to tell their own story. That is what American teachers and
parents need to hear most. It will make it easier to do what they
ultimately must do for and by themselves—to shape a better plan
for dealing with children before they go to school.

We are Lenin's Grandchildren
We are not yet Pioneers
We are not yet Octobrists,
But we know who we are for sure:
We are Lenin's Grandchildren!
We are Lenin's Grandchildren!

—Soviet kindergarten song

·I·

How It Started

IF YOUR CHILD lives to be a hundred, he will never again go through a period of such tumultuous physical, mental and moral development as in the period from birth to the age of seven. Some scientists believe that the important mental patterns are set in the first six years and can be changed later only with great difficulty, if at all. Yet, most educational systems leave this critical period of development to chance. The Soviet Union has developed an extraordinary program of preschool education, covering every phase of the young child's personality and designed to prevent the fears, inadequacies and cultural deprivations which handicap so many American students in the primary grades.

My interest in Soviet education began in 1960, when I was asked to join an adult Russian class, given by the Russian-born French teacher of the small private school located in Middleburg, Virginia, where my husband and I live. I found the language difficult, but fascinating. One by one the other students in the class dropped out, until only a friend and I were left. The class met once a week and only in winter, so our progress was not rapid; but by the end of the second year we were able to read Russian with the help of a dictionary. My friend subscribed to *Novaya Vremya* (*New Times*), and I subscribed to *Pravda* through a Russian bookstore in Washington, D. C. We exchanged reading matter, often on Sundays in the little Episcopal church we both attended.

In 1963 when the members of the Federal Bar Association and their families were invited to be guests of the government of

West Berlin for three days, my husband and I decided to go. To get our first look at the Soviet Union, we planned to fly to Leningrad after the official Berlin visit.

Our first encounter with Russians came in East Berlin, which we visited on the second day of the trip. The people on the streets were strangely quiet. Their faces showed no emotion, except, as we imagined, fear. There were soldiers everywhere. We got out of our bus to look at a Soviet monument and as we walked up to read the inscription my husband nudged me.

"Soviet soldiers," he said. "You can try out your Russian."

I turned and looked into a dozen impassive faces, unmistakably Soviet. "Go ahead," my husband said. "Talk to them." I gave my husband a wild look as though he were pushing me before a firing squad, but I walked up to the soldiers.

"Hello," I said in Russian, and the men jumped as though I had stabbed them with a bayonet. Then they gathered around me, all talking at once in such rapid Russian that I had no idea what they were saying. They began pulling snapshots out of their pockets—a picture of a plump woman, one of a little boy, pictures of little girls in stiff tarlatan hair ribbons, of babies in baby carriages, of babies swaddled like bundles for parcel post.

"*Detsky sad,*" one soldier said, pointing to a picture of his little boy. *Detsky*—children's, I translated; *sad*—garden. I couldn't understand. "What?" I asked. "*Shkola,*" he said.

"It's some kind of school his little boy goes to," I told my husband. "*Detsky sad.* I don't know just what it is."

The bus driver blew his horn and we ran for the bus, the soldiers running after us, laughing and shouting to us in Russian. They all waved goodbye as though we were old friends.

My first personal contact with Soviet education came as a result of a game of tennis. On the way from Berlin to Leningrad, we noticed another American on the plane with us, and, like us, he carried a tennis racket. When we asked him where he expected to play, he said he had no idea but had simply brought his racket in case courts were available. He said his name was Bud Chandler and that he was a lawyer from San Francisco.

When we arrived in Leningrad, two attractive Russian girls met us. "My name is Ludmila," one said to us in perfect English, while the other girl told Bud her name was Vera and that they were our guides for our stay in Leningrad. For the next few days the five of us went sightseeing together, admiring the beautiful old pastel-colored buildings reflected in the waters of the Neva River. Finally Bud and my husband asked the guides if there was any place to play tennis.

"We have never before had a tourist who wanted to play tennis," Ludmila said. "I'll ask Intourist." The Soviet tourist agency claimed that there was no place available, but Ludmila had an athletic cousin who gave us directions to a large sports complex where there were beautiful tennis courts. Two men dressed in long blue-jersey track suits offered to play tennis with Bud and my husband. My own tennis proved to be a problem. The only women players were international tournament players. Women who do not play tennis any better than I do simply do not play tennis in the Soviet Union. I was sent to practice on the backboard with the children.

The children were in the charge of a blond girl who demonstrated the strokes and then stood back and watched as the children rallied the ball against the backboard. There were about fifteen children, mostly boys between the ages of six and twelve. They were batting the balls very solemnly against an enormous backboard, and when I joined them they simply moved over to make room for me on the court, showing no emotion or surprise at my presence. When I hit a ball over the backboard, a boy who had also hit one over got my ball and tossed it to me as he picked up his own.

"*Vot* [Here]," he said, and went on batting the ball against the backboard.

The blond teacher put her hand on the arm of the boy next to me and swung his racket through a wide arc. She glanced at me and I swung as she had shown the boy. She nodded approvingly and turned to a small boy who was biting his lip in concentration every time he swung his racket. I was impressed with the concentration all the children showed. No one dawdled or interfered with another child. Finally the period was over and we all stopped. The children went off to other activities, and I returned to our guide.

"The children have to be able to hit the ball well before they are allowed to actually play tennis," Ludmila said. "They start every new game with exercises to strengthen the proper muscles. Then they learn the basic motions of the game, and when they have practiced these often enough they are finally allowed to play a real game. Educators feel that children are more apt to continue with a game if they know how to play it well. There are many of these sports centers, so children can play games after school at a center near their apartment. The Soviet Union is very interested in the health and physical perfection of the people."

I began to notice the children more after my tennis lesson. There was a park across the street from our hotel, and there always seemed to be children running around the statue of Pushkin in the center of the park. There were many old women sitting on park benches watching a particular child run around or dig in the park with a little shovel. Sometimes the old women pushed baby carriages, and occasionally we saw a younger

woman sitting by a carriage listening to a transistor radio resting in the carriage with the baby.

We saw groups of little children on the streets too, holding on to one another's coat tail as they crossed the street in a body. Sometimes a grownup held one end of a rope which passed through the children's hands to the other end held by another grown person. The children swayed across the street like a group of natives crossing a rope bridge over the Andes. The children's clothes were brighter and more stylishly made than the clothes of most of the grownups we saw.

There were groups of children in all the museums and parks we visited, listening intently as a teacher or guide explained that Lenin said this, or that "In the Soviet Union . . ."

Moscow was not as pretty as Leningrad, but it had an air of excitement that Leningrad lacked. Red Square was impressive, and the Kremlin dazzling. I wished I could remember more about Russian history.

We wondered about the people too—how they lived, how they brought up their children, what their hopes and fears were. We were delighted when our Moscow guide said, "Would you like to see a Soviet wedding?" We certainly would.

We were driven to a large, green building called a "Wedding Palace," a part of ZAGS, the agency for registering marriages. The front door opened into a vestibule with a small reception room on each side of it; the guide said these were "waiting" rooms, for grooms on one side and for brides on the other. The grooms sat nervously shrugging their coat sleeves into place and tugging at them with their hands.

Piped organ music boomed throughout the building as we went up a large staircase to a big room on the second floor, where there were rows of chairs on either side of the room and a desk at one end. We sat down and in a few minutes a woman in a tailored uniform came in and arranged a registration book and some papers on the desk. She nodded to us and then opened the door for the bride and groom. The bride carried three dahlias from whose stems the leaves had not been stripped. The leaves hung limp and dejected, and the dahlias themselves were beginning to wilt a little around the edges. Two girls, dressed in white, followed the bride, each carrying three zinnias with similarly wilted leaves on wet stems.

The bride was a plump, serious-looking girl with glasses and was dressed in a white knitted dress with a flat collar and a row of buttons down the center of her shirtwaist. The groom wore an ill-fitting suit and was continually rescuing his hands from the long sleeves of his jacket.

Among the wedding guests were two older women, presumably the bride's mother and the groom's mother, and a tanned,

white-haired man with a long white mustache, who evidently was the bride's father. There were two young men with the two bridesmaids, and three other people who were relatives or guests. All nodded to us and did not seem to mind our being there.

The woman in the uniform was joined by another uniformed woman, who busied herself with papers on the desk as the first official stepped forward to greet the young couple. The piped music began to play a wedding march. The official opened a book, which was definitely not a Bible, and began to read in a pleasant voice.

"We hope for your sake, that your marriage will be blessed with children," she said. "Children will add to your happiness. But more important, the state hopes you will raise socially useful citizens, because any marriage under the Soviet system is a union affecting not only the two participants but also the common interests of the society and of the government."

Three weeks was too short for anything more than a very fleeting impression, but I felt that I had to learn more about this country and its people. Toward the end of our visit to the Soviet Union, we were walking down a street in Kiev, near our hotel. I noticed a sign on the building. *"Detsky Sad,"* it said, and I remembered the picture the soldier in Berlin had shown me of his little boy. The windows of the building were at street level, and we could look down to a basement room filled with children, who were dressing, the older children helping the younger ones put their dresses and suits on over their underwear. We stared in at the children until a woman in a white lab coat looked up and saw us. She scowled and motioned us to go away.

"Detsky sad," I said, as we walked on. "Of course! It's a kindergarten!"

When we got home, our friends asked to see the pictures my husband had taken on our trip. They were particularly interested in the pictures of Soviet children. "Why, they look just like *our* children," they said in surprise, as though living under a different political system would somehow change the children visibly. The idea intrigued me. Were Soviet children different from American children?

To find the answer I went back to college. I enrolled in the graduate department of Russian-area studies at a university in Washington, D.C., where I studied Russian and Soviet history, Russian and Soviet literature, Russian civilization, Marxism, Russian intellectual thought of the nineteenth century, Soviet economic history, Soviet foreign policy, and other subjects related to Russia.

My friends responded as they would to any enthusiast they knew. When they ran into a Russian somewhere they called me to meet him. Russians turned up in the oddest places. A Soviet scientist appeared at a Rappahannock fox hunt. A Soviet general paid a visit to a friend of ours who was an American general in an exchange called "Arms for Friendship." A friend who was an editor of *Holiday* Magazine introduced us to the editor of *Soviet Life,* the English-language magazine the Soviets send us in return for our *Amerika* written in Russian. My Russian was getting better and my knowledge of the background of Soviet affairs was much broader, but there was so much to learn. We needed to make another trip to the Soviet Union.

Our 1965 trip was longer and more varied. We covered eight

On later visits to a detsky sad, *with proper introductions, everyone was smiling.*

of the fifteen republics of the Soviet Union—Kazakh, Tadzhik, Uzbek, Georgia, Armenia, Russia, Ukraine, and Azerbaijzhan. (In 1967 and 1969 we added three more—Byelorussia, Turkmenia and Moldavia.) We saw for ourselves the vastness of a country which covers one sixth of the world's land mass, but more important, in 1967, we made our first official visit to a kindergarten in Moscow. My own education about the children of the Soviet Union was beginning.

·II·

The Privileged Class

IT WASN'T AN imposing neighborhood, even by Moscow standards—just row after row of identical apartment houses, with angular balconies jutting out squarely from each apartment. Most balconies were decorated with flowers in pots, but the flowers, many now frost-blackened, were too small to distract from the generally austere air of the buildings.

The ground floors of the apartments were occupied by small shops, and here and there, the sign *"Gastronom"* announced a grocery store. The dirt roads around the buildings were dry and dusty now, but a good rain would turn them into mud. All of the buildings seemed to have been built in too much of a hurry, but here they were, big, ugly and unapologetic. The Russians call this complex a "microblock"—which means that there are factories, schools, stores, playgrounds, a Palace of Culture and medical services, all within easy reach.

The school itself was a plain, two-story brick building with a ring of trees around it, a playground on one side, and a small vegetable garden, abandoned for the winter, on the other side. The director of the school, a pretty woman in her early forties, with short, dark hair and a clear skin, was waiting outside to meet us.

"Welcome," she said, in Russian. "We are honored to have you with us."

"We call this a *kombinat*," the director explained. "That means that we have both *yasli* [nursery school] and *detsky sad* [kindergarten]. We don't have many little babies here; just three under a year old. Our *yasli* group—the children under

The author, second from left, and teaching staff in front of a typical detsky sad *in Ashkabad.*

three—consists of thirty children now, including the babies, though this varies from time to time and also varies from school to school. My sister teaches in a large *kombinat* with two hundred and eighty children, eighty of whom are in *yasli*. In most schools the largest concentration of children is in the four-to-seven-year-old groups. First grade starts at seven."

"Our children start school at six," I said. "Is your last year of kindergarten like our first grade?"

"In the past, we thought the six-year-old too young for regular school work," the director said, leading us into her small, neat office, where she hung our coats on a wooden coat tree. "Some schools are now teaching reading and counting, whereas formerly they only taught reading readiness, but the *podgotovka-k-shkole* (preparation-for-school) group is still not treated like a regular school class. They play more and take naps during the day, which first-graders don't do."

"Since this school combines both nursery and kindergarten children, we have four groups, with ten teachers, plus a musical director. We have thirty people in all on our staff to care for a hundred children." She paused, speculatively, "I don't know why we were chosen for you to visit. There is nothing special about our school. There are much finer ones in other sections." She said this in a matter-of-fact way without sounding apologetic.

"We love our children," the director said, leading us up some stairs. "We call the children our privileged class, because we try to give them the best of what we have. We haven't always had so much—we lost twenty million people and many of our cities in the last war alone. The children are our future, and we want that future to be a happy one."

At the head of the stairs we turned left into a large, well-lighted room, where fifteen three-year-olds sat on small wooden chairs around matching tables. In the front of the room, a teacher, a pretty young girl in a pale-yellow sweater and dark-gray woolen skirt, her blond hair piled on top of her head, was making paper airplanes by inserting wings into slits which she had made in the folded bodies. In the background a solid woman of forty or so acted as the teacher's helper. The helper wore a white lab coat with sleeves rolled up over two powerful arms; she smiled broadly at us when we entered. The teacher also smiled, but the three-year-olds looked serious and interested.

All the children had short hair, the boys in crew cuts and the girls in Dutch bobs, to which, with some difficulty, big white tarlatan hair bows had been secured. The children were well dressed in attractive, bright-colored rompers or dresses. They had the same well-scrubbed look as the building.

My husband moved to a far corner to get pictures, and the director and I stepped a little closer into the room.

"*Zdravstvuite* [Hello]," the director said to the group.

"*Zdravstvuite*," the group replied in a chorus, a thumb-sucking boy managing to join in without dislodging his thumb from his mouth.

The director looked at the thumb-sucker. "We try to discourage that," she said. "This child is new here and did not go to nursery school. He's a little behind the others. We have to work harder on such children."

The teacher handed a little boy an airplane and nodded toward us. The boy with shoulders back but head down, marched up and put the plane in my hand. I thanked him, and he grinned broadly, hunching up his shoulders in pleasure, and returned to his seat.

"I want to give them one," a little girl whispered loudly to the teacher.

"I do too," another child said.

One by one the children came over and each gave me a plane. Some handed their present up quickly and ducked back to their seats. Others presented the plane solemnly as though they were precious jewels. All were well behaved and seemed to enjoy the performance. I was so interested in the procedure that I completely forgot that I had a present for them.

When the children had returned to their chairs, the teacher opened a book to read the story of Komar Komarovich (*komar* is the word for "mosquito") with the long nose and Misha, the hairy bear with the short tail.

"It happened just at noon," the teacher read, and the children leaned forward intently. "All the mosquitoes were hiding from the heat in the swamp. Komar Komarovich Long Nose was snoozing on a leaf, when suddenly he heard a shout.

" 'Oy, good gracious! Oy, help.'

" 'What happened?' Komar Komarovich Long Nose wanted to know.

" 'Oy, good gracious! A bear came in our swamp and lay down to sleep. As he lay down in the grass he crushed fifty mosquitoes; and as he breathed he swallowed a hundred whole. Oh, there is trouble ahead, brothers!' "

The children held their breath in excitement. The teacher showed them a picture of a bear lying in the thick grass with a mosquito standing on his nose. The mosquito was waving a long sword at the bear, who had his mouth open.

Misha, the bear, is the most popular story character and the most popular toy.

"Hairy Misha opened one eye. He didn't see anything," The teacher read on. "He opened the other eye. He could barely see that the mosquito had flown onto his very own nose."

The children did not even look up at us as we tiptoed out of the room and the teacher continued to read as though she were auditioning for a role at the Moscow Art Theater. She seemed as intent on the story as the children were.

"What happened to the bear?" my husband wanted to know.

When I translated his question, the director said calmly, "Komar Komarovich chased him out of the swamp." She was not surprised at the question.

. . .

In the next room were several cribs with very young babies in them. A nurse was standing by one crib exercising a baby. He was lying on his back while the nurse moved his arms and legs rhythmically and then carefully pulled him to a sitting position.

"Many parents think their babies are too young to understand anything at this age," the director said. "But, even at birth, the child has organs of feeling. He can distinguish sour from sweet, he shows uneasiness at strong odors, and when cold, he begins to cry."

In another crib a four-month-old baby was lying quietly

contemplating her toes, when a nurse came over and dangled a bright red toy in front of her.

"Look. Look here, Yanka," the nurse called to the baby, and Yanka stared at the red toy. As the nurse moved the toy from left to right, Yanka's eyes followed the movement.

"Yanka is showing what we call the 'spectator function,'" the director said. "Pavlov said it starts with the curiosity reflex. This same curiosity reflex will make the child ask 'What is that?' when she can talk, and later on she will want to know 'Why?'"

The nurse was smiling at Yanka and talking to her as she showed her the toy. "Give me your hand, Yanka." Yanka was delighted. With unintelligible Russian gurgles, she grabbed the nurse's finger and smiled.

"When they come to us at two months they should be able to look at a grownup attentively and respond to vocal or musical sounds, and should smile in response to a smiling adult," the director explained. "They should make energetic movements and happy sounds as Yanka is doing now. This emotional reaction is important, as it strengthens the musculature and forms mental connections between speech and physical activities."

As we left Yanka and stepped out into the corridor, a husky lab-coated attendant pulled my husband to one side and motioned for him to follow her, at the same time pointing to his cameras. My husband knows no Russian but will follow a picture lead anywhere, so he immediately went off with his new guide, who quickly led him into a room at the end of the corridor.

"She wants him to take pictures of *her* children," the director explained to me. "She is very fond of them and would be hurt if we missed them."

We followed through the door onto a sleeping veranda, where my husband was already busy photographing the sleeping children. The room was full of small white iron beds arranged head to foot in closely placed rows. The beds had gray woolen blankets bordered with dark-green pine trees and nursery-type animals. Only six of the beds were occupied, and their occupants were sound asleep. The white pillows of the unoccupied beds were propped up at a rakish angle like sails in a high wind.

"Our youngest," the director said. "At this age they spend a lot of time sleeping, although in any group you will find some who won't sleep in the daytime."

"Is this normal?" I asked.

"No. It is because some grown person has made a mistake with the child. He has strengthened the wrong habits. You can tell how a child will sleep by the way it plays. A happy child will go to sleep much faster than an unhappy one."

The next room we were shown was an indoor playroom full of toys. In a playpen a baby, just able to sit up, looked around vacantly and teetered unsteadily. The nurse brought another baby of apparently the same age and sat the stranger in the pen facing the other child. The director motioned for us to watch.

"We want the children not only to learn to play but to play together. This is the beginning of collectivism, which is the basis of our system," the director said.

For a few moments nothing much happened in the playpen. The first baby stared at the newcomer, and the newcomer stared back. Both rocked back and forth jerkily. We watched for some further signs of collectivism. The first baby picked up a red plastic duck which was lying nearby and put it into his mouth, chewing on it reflectively. The second baby continued to stare, and his pupils grew larger and dark, then he smiled and said something in Russian baby talk that sounded like "Goo."

"A splendid beginning," the director said, leaning over the pen and picking up the second baby. *Molodets* [Good boy]," she whispered in the baby's ear and handed him over to the nurse.

The director turned back to us. "We don't want to try his endurance too far. A smile is the best we can hope for on the first collective enterprise."

"Do they always get along all right?" I asked.

"Oh, no. Sometimes they throw things at each other, or cry at the sight of the strange child. Gradually they get used to having other children around and then they learn to enjoy one another's company."

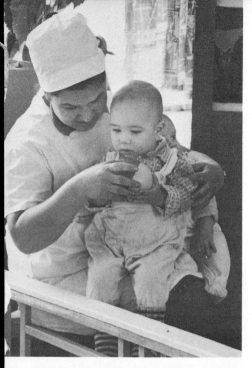

Children's society must be organized, say the Soviets, and in their education they stress moral experience through collective activities. At left, neatly balancing two babies on her lap, a young teacher introduces them to a red-and-white ball. Later, they will be placed in a common playpen (as in the photo below) to begin the development of a good "collective relationship."

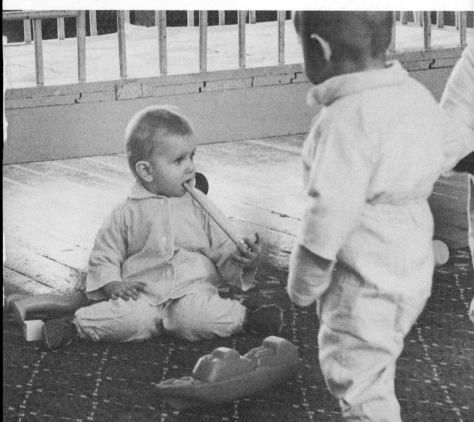

Returning to the street level, we walked past the bathrooms equipped with small washbasins, across from which were hung the towels. Over each towel was a picture of an animal, which identified a child's towel for him.

We went on to the kitchen, where a plump middle-aged woman with an oilcloth apron with a bib was bending over a large mixing bowl, making a pastry called *pirozhki*. She had a white cotton cap on her head and also wore boots. Through the door we could see a pantry piled high with all kinds of foods.

The dining room, next to the kitchen, had small tables and the same highly scrubbed look of everything in the school. On the wall was a large bulletin board, which the director called the "wall newspaper," giving the day's schedule for each age group. We read the schedule for the five-to-six-year-olds and noted that it also gave directions for the parents to follow before and after the school day.

The children were to arrive at the kindergarten around 7:30 A.M., and a nurse immediately took their temperatures and checked them for health problems. If the check was satisfactory, they played and had morning gymnastics until 8:30, when they were given breakfast. Various activities, including a walk, occupied them until 12:30 P.M., when they were given dinner. After dinner, a nap was prescribed. More play, another walk, and the school day ended at 7 P.M.

Preschool institutions are required, under Soviet law, to be built in every apartment-house complex, collective farm or factory employing women. Normally, one of the parents drops the child off on the way to work and picks him up in the evening on the way back. Many of the schools have facilities for keeping some children overnight, so that these can remain at the school if parents are able to care for them only on weekends or vacations.

The wall newspaper included the school menus for the week, so that parents could avoid duplicating the school's offerings when they fed their children supper at home. We looked over a sample menu:

BREAKFAST:
Hot dish
Tea, Milk, Coffee with Milk

DINNER:
First course: Soup
Second course: Meat Cutlet
Garniture: Vegetable or Kasha [1]
Third course: Compote or Kisel [2]

SNACK:
Fruit juice, Tea, Coffee, Milk
Pastry or Roll

SUPPER:
Kasha, Vegetables, etc.
Milk, Kisel, Compote

The sizes of portions were also specified in grams, one size for the three-to-five and another for the five-to-seven age group. In the kitchen we had seen a chart giving the amount of water to be added to various forms of *kasha.* We were amazed at the variety of the list: buckwheat, millet, rice, pearl barley, oatmeal, semolina, wheat, lentils, peas and beans. The children were definitely assured of variety in their *kasha.*

"The teachers are entitled to one meal a day," the director explained. "They may eat with the children or in a separate dining room if they prefer."

The left side of the wall newspaper constituted the "Parents' Corner," a standard feature in Soviet nurseries and kindergartens. In addition to news of parent committee meetings the Parents' Corner contained references to articles which the parents were advised to read; books suitable for reading to the children; and bulletins on childhood ailments. There was also a

[1] A porridgelike cereal preparation, most commonly of buckwheat or millet.
[2] A kind of pudding made of fruit and a starchy flour.

Parents' Corner in Tashkent. Each child's weight and height is reported regularly. The menu for the week is also included. Books for parents are recommended, as well as those to be read to the child. Among the suggestions is one that the parents listen to the child when he returns from school.

clipping from *Pravda* showing a happy buxom woman receiving a Motherland Glory medal after giving birth to her ninth child.

Noticing my interest in the clipping, the director explained: "Mothers who have borne and brought up five or six children receive motherhood medals. For seven to nine children the Motherland Glory medal is awarded and for ten the Mother Heroine."

Pausing for a moment after leaving the wall newspaper, we looked through the window at the light snow that was falling. Some of the older children were playing outside under an attendant's watchful eyes. They were trying hard to scrape up enough snow to build a snowman, but the effort was doomed to failure. It was still too early in the season. We noticed that the play area was equipped with swings, slides and a sandbox, all collecting a light icing of white.

We went upstairs again and into a class of twenty children between the ages of five and six. The teacher was holding up a picture and telling the children to look at it closely. Next she held up another picture, which at first glance seemed to be the same as the previous one.

"What has changed?" she asked. "Can you tell me how this picture is different from the first picture?" The children were thinking so hard that they did not notice us. The director interrupted.

"Children, here are Mr. and Mrs. Weaver all the way from America. Do you know where America is?"

"*Da, Da* [Yes, Yes]." The children looked up, staring at us with interest. One child immediately came up to us and gave us a limp little hand.

"*Zdravstvuite,*" he said solemnly, as we shook hands.

Suddenly all the children got up and surrounded us. We had completely disrupted the class, but the teacher did not seem to mind. The children were not crowding too close to us, and there was no pushing or shouting. I still had the jigsaw puzzle which I had brought as a present, under my arm. I handed the puzzle to a boy who had noticed it, and suddenly all the little hands in the room reached for the present.

The teacher took the puzzle, and as she picked it up two pieces tumbled out onto the floor. The teacher's face turned scarlet, and for a moment she seemed on the verge of panic. Obviously, she thought she had broken our gift.

I showed her how to put it back together and explained how the children could play with it. She was dubious at first, apparently, never having seen such a jigsaw puzzle before, but when she put it down on the table and saw how the pieces fitted together to make a picture, she was very pleased.

One boy brought me a pile of drawings, and the children stood around me as I looked at them. The drawings were of flowers and were exact enough so that I could tell what flowers they were: asters, zinnias, cosmos and goldenrod.

"Zinnia," the children said, as I turned to the first drawing.

"One, two, three, four, five flowers," a little girl counted, in Russian. The other children counted after her.

Some of the children had gathered around my husband to

have their pictures taken, and one boy cupped his hands over his eyes in imitation of the camera.

"We're disrupting your class," I apologized.

"We like for the children to meet people from other countries. This is the best way to teach internationalism, and internationalism is one of the themes of our October holiday. You came at an excellent time," the teacher said.

I was delighted with the children and didn't want to leave, but the director said it was time for the "matinee" performance.

We went into a large hall with a television set and an upright wooden piano at one end of the room, and small wooden chairs arranged along the other three walls. There were potted plants on the windowsills of the large windows, and across one wall was a bright-red banner with Lenin's picture in the middle and "50 *Let* [50 years]" written across the banner. Under Lenin's picture was a vase of fresh flowers. On a small table was a framed family portrait of Lenin as a child, with his brother, sister and mother. It was the kind of family picture almost any American family might have had on their living-room table.

We were introduced to the musical director, a slender girl in her twenties, with a shoulder-length page-boy bob of red hair, and wearing a dark-blue dress.

We took seats in the front row of chairs, and the musical director sat down at the piano and started to play "Moya Rodina [My Motherland]" as the children marched in, carrying red flags. The little girls had the same big white tarlatan hair bows

tied on short stiff locks of hair that we had seen on the other children earlier, and the boys had short hair. The girls wore stylish little dresses in different colors, and most of the boys were in short pants and shirts. The children took seats along one wall, sitting with their feet firmly on the floor, their hands folded in their laps or with one hand, palms down, resting on each knee. The children settled themselves in their chairs as the blond teacher stood up in front of them. "Everything is ready for the holiday," she said. "Look, the bus is bringing the little children. Let's greet them with a friendly song."

The musical director nodded at the seated children, her hands on the piano keys. As the children started to sing, there was a bustle at the door and a line of younger children came in, double file. The first two children wore cardboard headlights. Then came a little boy with a big cardboard steering wheel in his hands. Two children in each line carried round cardboard wheels with big tires painted on them, and the "passengers" carried the dark-blue paper sides of the bus under their outside arms.

The passengers sang:

> *One, two; left, right. We march with a song.*
> *No other holiday October has been as wonderful as this.*

The seated group of children sang back:

> *Holiday, holiday, holiday October!*
> *The flags, the flags, the red flags are exciting*
> *Faces are joyous, everyone is merry.*
> *The red flags are exciting.*

The bus pulled up to some empty chairs, and the passengers took seats along the wall. When everyone was seated there was a shout: "Long live the October holiday! Oorah!"

"The streets bloom with banners and flags and the people sing joyfully," the blond teacher said, as the children began to dance to the tune of a polka.

The music soon changed from a polka to a Russian dance. The little boys squatted down uncertainly, kicking their legs out somewhat shakily in the typical Cossack fashion. Everyone was a little out of breath when the dance was over. Some of the boys bowed to their partners, but most just forgot and sat down, as a girl in a pink dress recited a story about a bear.

The teacher called the children's attention to a toy kiosk in one corner of the room, from which she took hoops for a game to be played by the children who had not been in the dance. After the game was over, she took out a trumpet, held it to her lips and blew, but no sound came out. "Children," she said, "The trumpet won't play. Probably there is some obstruction here."

She put her hand into the end of the trumpet and pulled out

a brightly colored handkerchief. There was a murmur of surprise from the children, which changed to delight as the teacher pulled several more handkerchiefs from the trumpet. One boy rocked forward and clapped his hands. The dark little boy next to him watched tensely, his hands tightly clasped between his knees.

"That is a new boy," the director said, pointing to the dark child. "He has just transferred from a boarding school and is still very tense." The teacher handed the first handkerchief to the new boy, who looked surprised and pleased, then glanced at the teacher uncertainly as the other children with handkerchiefs got up and started to do a dance. The teacher placed a firm hand on the new boy's shoulder and guided him expertly into the dance. Whenever he made a wrong turn, her gentle hand set him straight, and he went back to his chair relaxed and confident, to watch a relay race between two groups of four-year-olds.

Two chairs were placed in the middle of the room, with a red scarf over the back of each chair. The children were divided into two teams under Sasha and Golya, who as captains had the first turns.

"One . . . two . . ." The teacher built up suspense as the children stiffened in expectation.

Suddenly it came: "Three!"

It caught Sasha by surprise. Golya was already running toward the chair, and Sasha was still at the starting line. He had to hurry. He slipped, but caught himself and ran on. Golya had reached his chair and picked up the scarf. He put it over his head, but in his hurry, he covered his face with it. The other children half rose from their chairs in suspense. Would he get it tied under his chin?

His face emerged from the folds of the scarf, but now his fingers would not work. The ends of the scarf kept slipping through his hands. Sasha had reached his chair, and with one deft movement tied his scarf around his head. Sasha, left at the post at the start, had won the race. The children clapped.

"Sasha went to nursery school, Golya didn't," the director whispered. "You can see the difference. *Yasli* children learn physical dexterity."

"*Molodets* [Good boy]," the musical director said softly to Golya as the boys took their seats and their teammates continued the race.

When the race was over the musical director said, "What song would you like to sing, children?"

"Grandfather Frost" . . . "Dancing Bear" . . . "There Will Always Be Mama," the children called out. After some discussion, "Mama" was chosen, and sweet, serious little voices sang:

> *May there always be sunshine,*
> *May there always be blue skies,*
> *May there always be Mama,*
> *May there always be me.*

The first part of the program concluded with a recitation, "Little Fir Tree," by four-year-old Tanya, who recited with a ham actor's delight at being the center of attention. She held her skirt with one hand, her little finger pointing out stiffly. At the end of her recitation the piano sounded the signal for the younger children to march out of the room. We could see Tanya was not satisfied with the exit. She and the teacher were having a discussion. In a minute the teacher came over and whispered to the director.

"Do you mind listening to Tanya again?" the director asked us. "She wants to do her piece once more. She is a very emotional child, and we try to give her special attention when she needs it."

Returning to the center of the room, Tanya began a new piece: "Today I went with Mama, along the boulevard—" She stopped suddenly as she noticed the little children filing out of the room. Her eyes filled with tears.

"She wants the other children to stay and listen to her," the director explained. "She is very temperamental, but this is too much." The director nodded to one of the white-uniformed nurses who went up to Tanya, put an arm around her, and leaned down to speak to her. The tears stopped, and Tanya seemed quite content with whatever it was the nurse proposed. She went out contentedly with the other three- and four-year-olds as the program continued with the older children.

"Who is coming to visit us?" the musical director said as six boys rode into the hall on tricycles.

"They must be collective farmers on their horses," the director said, as six girls in Russian costume went out to greet the boys:

We live in our native collective farm in friendly, happy fashion,
Together we sow, together we plow
Together we sing and dance.

The boys got off their velocipedes and did a dance with the girls, then the girls said, "We have some presents for you, but first you must guess some riddles."

> *Rosy cheeks, white nose*
> *In the darkness I sit all day,*
> *But the green jacket is all in the sunshine.*

"Radish!" the boys shouted, then listened intently to the next riddle: "One hundred coats, and all without a buckle."

"Cabbage!" the boys said.

The program continued, alternating lively games like "Flyer to the Airport" with quiet construction games like "Tuk-a-Tuk, We Build a House" and recitations:

> *Let there be peace*
> *In all the world,*
> *Let there be peace always,*
> *So that we may grow up*
> *For brave deeds,*
> *For happiness and work!*

When the program was over we walked back to the office with the director. "Suppose, through automation or otherwise, Soviet mothers were no longer needed in the labor force and could stay at home, would nurseries and kindergartens still be expanded?" my husband asked.

"Some mothers stay at home now," the director replied, "but our women would not be content with idleness. Even if women workers were not needed, our kindergartens and nurseries would still be necessary. Here we do things for the children that their parents are not trained or equipped to do."

The answer states a fact that is clearly apparent. The Soviet preschool program is much more than a device to free the mothers for work. It provides a nationwide, highly centralized, educational system for preschool children designed to produce the kind of citizen the Soviets feel is needed for the Communist world.

Social graces are emphasized in the dancing class, which is a standard feature of the Soviet preschool curriculum.

·III·

The System

THE GOALS AND POLICIES of the Soviet system of public education originate with the Central Committee of the Communist Party, whose resolutions are promulgated as decrees or laws of the Council of Ministers of the U.S.S.R., with or without ratification of the Supreme Soviet.

The Central Committee decides on a program, and an appropriate body is asked to investigate and make recommendations for specific implementation of the program. If there is no existing body deemed appropriate for such research, one is created. To respond to the growing interest in preschool education, the Scientific Research Institute of Preschool Education was created in 1960 as one of the research institutes of the Academy of Pedagogical Sciences, established in 1944.

The late A. P. Usova was selected to draw up a draft program of education in the kindergarten. Working with Dr. A. V. Zaporozhets, who was to head the Preschool Institute, and others from the Academy of Pedagogical Sciences and the Academy of Medical Science, she drew up a detailed program of instruction, or *vospitanie,* as opposed to *obuchenie.* (*Vospitanie* and *obuchenie* both mean educational instruction or training, but *vospitanie* is generally understood to mean "upbringing," as opposed to the formal study of specific subjects implied by *obuchenie.*) The *Program of Instruction in the Kindergarten,* developed from the earlier draft, was published in 1962 as a detailed, comprehensive manual of methods for implementing this goal. The *Program* was revised in 1965 and revised again in 1969. At the same time the primary grades, which had previously consisted of four years, were shortened to three years, presumably putting more pressure on the kindergarten to fill the gap. The preschool institutions are the foundation of a general system of public education. The child, who may have started *yasli* at two months of age, will continue through kindergarten (from three years of age through six), enter first grade at seven for three years of primary grades, then go to the middle, or secondary, school of eight or ten years. (The three or four years of primary school are included in the eight- or ten-year period). Under Khrushchev an eleven-year school was started, and there are still a few of these left, though the eleven-year school was never universally adopted.

At present the eight-year secondary school is compulsory, and the goal is to make the ten-year school compulsory in the future. When the student graduates from the eight- or ten-year school, between the ages of fourteen and nineteen, he may go to a three-year technical school, or two- or three-year teacher's college, or directly to a job. Even for those who continue higher education, a year or two of work experience before university is quite common, and those with work experience are often given preferential treatment. The term "higher school" refers to university training and not to "high school" as we know it in the United States. Soviet schools are in a constant state of change in a perpetual effort at improvement, and since the changes do not always occur simultaneously throughout the Soviet Union, the older forms persist in some places while the new ones are instituted in others.

Moscow, as the home of the Preschool Institute and as the home office of the Party, is usually the first with the new. Thus, it is not surprising that this city should be the first to require children entering school in 1970 or after either to attend kindergarten or to take remedial courses on entering the first grade, to catch up with the children who have attended kindergarten. Actually, in a typical Moscow first grade, most of the children have gone to kindergarten anyhow, so the new regulations will not be much of a hardship.

In large cities like Moscow and Leningrad, about eighty

percent of preschool-age children go to *detsky sad,* and about forty percent go to *yasli.* In some rural areas the percentage of attendance may be as low as twenty percent for kindergartens. At present there are not enough places to meet the demand and there are waiting lists for most kindergartens, despite the continued building of new ones.

In Kazakhstan before the Revolution, there was not a single preschool institution. The first was built in 1917; and by 1921 there were 115 kindergartens in Kazakhstan. At the beginning of the twentieth century seventy-six percent of the Russian people were illiterate. Only seven tenths of one percent of the Turkmenian people could read and write. Today, the Soviet Union is practically one-hundred-percent literate.

In 1960 there were 43,600 preschool institutions in the Soviet Union, with 3,115,100 pupils. By 1965 this had grown to 67,500 schools and 6,207,300 pupils. The total number of children in *yasli* and *detsky sad* is expected to reach twelve million in 1970 or soon after.

Unlike the primary and secondary schools, the *yasli* and *detsky sad* are neither compulsory nor free. The *yasli,* which is under the Department of Health, and the *detsky sad* and *kombinat* (including the *yasli* part of the *kombinat*) which are under the Department of Education, are financed from the national budget, with each preschool institution having its own budget, and like other Soviet institutions, its own goals to fulfill. The school budget is part of the over-all Union budget as well as a part of the budget of each individual republic. Each of the fifteen Soviet republics which make up the Soviet Union also has its own minister of education. In 1966 Mikhail Prokofyev became the first U.S.S.R. minister of education, though the individual republics retain their own ministers.

Seventy-five or eighty percent of the cost of *yasli* and *detsky sad* is borne by the state. The amount a parent pays is determined by a number of factors. Mothers earning up to sixty rubles a month and having two children receive a twenty-five percent reduction. Those having three children and earning up to forty rubles get a fifty percent reduction. Those with three children and earning up to eighty rubles a month receive a thirty-five percent reduction, and those with four or more children, regardless of their earnings, receive a fifty percent reduction in school fees.

Further reductions are made if either the child or the parent is ill for more than three days. Considerations such as alimony, pensions, state grants, and other forms of income are also weighed in determining the fee. In special cases, a parent's trade union may help with preschool tuition costs.

In most cases the fees amount to between three and twelve rubles a month. They are to be paid a month in advance and not later than the tenth of the month. If the bill is not paid within two weeks after it falls due, the child is dismissed from his school.

Just as the *Program of Instruction* outlines the methods to be used in the upbringing of the children, the *Handbook of Preschool Education* explicitly defines details of buildings, equipment and personnel. The *Handbook* discusses the type of light bulbs to be used as thoroughly as it discusses settlements of work disputes among employees. Our visits to schools in eleven of the fifteen republics showed that the guidelines of the *Handbook* were followed strictly.

The school buildings are generally one or two stories of brick or stucco with large windows. They are scrupulously clean, even though some of the older buildings have chipped stair treads or cracks in the walls. The newer buildings are modern, with great expanses of glass. Their façades are decorated with designs illustrating fairy tales or the national symbol of one of the republics.

Outside there is always a "green plantation." No less than fifty percent of the whole plot must be allotted to gardens and playgrounds. Usually there is a berry patch, a vegetable garden and a small fruit orchard. The playgrounds are well equipped with swings, climbing equipment, slides, sandboxes and a playhouse. Some schools also have swimming pools or wading pools. Most have at least a small fountain or pool for what the Soviets call "water procedure" (sailing boats and playing with water toys). Some kindergartens have large wooden models of moon

(Above) Water play is a regular outdoor activity and coeducational activities are especially encouraged (Tashkent, Kombinat 208). (Below) A "green plantation" and playground outside a typical school building, this one in Sochi.

rockets in which the children can play. The whole complex is enclosed by a wrought-iron fence or a colorfully decorated cement-block wall.

Cement walks around the school are available for game playing, but most of the children seem to prefer the mud that the winter snows and spring rains leave in the schoolyards. Since the children wear the *valenki,* felt boots with rubber bottoms, they are well protected from the cold and wet, and no one forbids them to play in the mud.

Inside the buildings the rooms are large and pleasant. There is a reception room, a play-dining room, a music hall, a sleeping veranda, toilets, kitchen, storage rooms, laundry room, and an office for the *zaveduyushaya* (director) and a dining room and rest rooms for the staff.

The school may be simply a day school, with the children arriving between seven and nine in the morning and going home between four and seven in the evening, or it may be a five-day school, where the children spend only weekends at home, usually going home Saturday around noon and returning Sunday night or Monday morning. Some day pupils also go to school on Saturday mornings in addition to the five weekdays. The Soviet Union only recently adopted a five-day work week for most of its adult workers, so some kindergartens have not yet adapted to a five-day week. Sometimes a school will have a small group which stays at night after the rest of the children go home. There are also facilities for parents who need to leave their child just for a night or two. Arrangements are quite flexible, depending upon the schedule of the parents.

Some kindergartens are organized as separate institutions, some are connected with industries and factories, and some are connected with cooperatives and collective farms. Nursing mothers who work are encouraged to put their babies in a *yasli* connected with their factory, and they are given time off to nurse their babies and to play and talk with them. Early weaning is discouraged, and a relaxed, pleasant relationship between mother and child is encouraged. In collective farms and rural areas there are often seasonal *yasli*s for mothers who do only part-time work. All *yasli*s and *detsky sad*s must be registered in accordance with the regional or town department of people's education.

In a *yasli* the children are usually divided into three groups. The first group is subdivided into infants from two to six months, six to nine months, and nine or ten months to one year. The other two *yasli* groups are for children of one to two, and two to three.

In a *detsky sad* there are usually four groups, with the youngest (*mladshaya*) group consisting of children from three to four years, the middle (*srednaya*) group of children of four and five, the older (*starshaya*) group of five-year-olds and the preparation-for-school (*podgotovka-k-shkole*) group of six-year-olds.

The schools are designed for groups of 90, 140 and 280. Most of the buildings are planned so that each room gets the maximum amount of sunlight.

There are special kindergartens for blind, deaf and mute children, and children with diseases of the central nervous system, as well as special kindergartens conducted in some foreign language. The English-language kindergartens are especially popular (though difficult to enter), and the child may go on to an English-language primary and secondary school as well. In such schools English is spoken entirely, and Russian is taught as a foreign language.

The transfer of children from one group to the next usually takes place between August 25 and September 15 each year. September 1 is the official opening day for regular school. Each school child carries a bouquet of flowers to the teacher on opening day; so, on that day the streets of towns and cities resemble a moving flower show.

The director, at the head of the kindergarten must have had at least a pedagogical-college education, or a general education with special pedagogical courses and no less than two years' practical work in a kindergarten. In the *yasli,* the director must have had a higher-school special education.

The director, almost always a woman, is responsible for hiring teachers, filling pupil vacancies, following the hygienic rules laid down by the government and, in general, creating favorable conditions for furthering the welfare of her pupils. She must be concerned with increasing the general and political level of development and the educational qualifications of the teachers. She sees that the school is supplied with toys, which are kept in good repair, organizes parents' committees, sees that vegetables and fruits are properly stored for winter so that they retain their vitamin content, supervises all workers in the school and makes out a yearly report to be presented to the Department of Public Education.

In addition to the director, there is a music leader, who must have had a special musical education. The music director assists the teachers with the children in singing, physical culture, and preparation for the children's holiday celebrations.

There is also a doctor, who is hired or fired by the head doctor of the region in which the kindergarten is located. In the Soviet Union the majority of doctors are women, and this is particularly true in the preschool institutions. The doctor is responsible for such prophylactic measures as disinfection, quarantine, and isolation of the sick. She takes children who need special care to the polyclinic or local hospital, is responsible for the sanitation of the school, and controls the work in physical education.

In a large school the doctor may have a *feldsher* as assistant; or, if the school is too small for a full time doctor, the *feldsher* may serve in place of the doctor. There is a medical nurse who checks the throat and skin of each child daily, and a practical nurse (or a number of them) who, though without pedagogic or medical education, is the backbone of the school, especially for the *yasli* group.

Pravda and *Uchitelskaya Gazeta* (*Teacher's Newspaper*) are often concerned that these goodhearted practical nurses are looked down upon by the more highly educated teachers and ordered around without even a *pozhaluista* ("please").

The service staff of the kindergarten consists of a cook, kitchen helpers, laundresses, maids, furnaceman, gardeners and draymen, all of whom seem particularly interested in their jobs. The

"Bread in left hand, spoon in right hand. No talking with mouth full"
is the rule at each of the three meals daily served each child (Moscow,
Kindergarten No. 1914).

school kitchens were all immaculate, with shining stainless-steel
kettles bubbling with aromatic soup which tasted as good as it
smelled. The meals we had in kindergartens, whether with children or with teachers, were better than those we had in the best
hotel. Lunch usually consisted of soup, meat cutlets, vegetables,
and fruit compote, with bread and milk.

To help the work of the schools and to check on the progress
of the work there is a "cabinet of methodists and inspectors."
Each region (Moscow, for example, is divided into thirty regions) has a head inspector and from three to five methodists.

The methodist cabinet supervises and checks on the qualifications of all preschool workers, gives courses for older teachers
and musical directors to keep them up to date, and arranges
demonstrations and exhibits as well as coordinating information

from other institutions and updating the course of study in the *yasli* and *detsky sad.*

In large regions, individual methodists specialize in particular fields. One methodist will work with speech problems in a whole region, while another is occupied with methods of drawing. If the *kombinat* has more than six groups it will have its own methodist. Otherwise there are about three methodists for each sixty-five preschool institutions.

Leningrad, which is divided into nineteen districts, has one inspector and two methodists for each region. The inspector controls the work of the preschool institution and helps to improve it; sees that directives and decisions of the Party and government, as well as orders from the Ministry of Education, are followed in the schools. She is familiar with the Program of preschool instruction as well as the recommendations of the preschool methodist cabinet. Since it is impossible to inspect each class every time, the inspector relies a great deal on the director. The director usually tells her which teachers need help, how they live, and what they read.

The inspector is interested in the relations of the teachers with one another and with the children, and the relations of the children with one another. She checks furniture, laundry, toys, books and work of the kindergarten as a whole, and when she sees some insufficiency she sets out to correct it through conversation with the teachers and directors. Often her observations lead to recommendations for changes in the general system as well as in a particular school. She must be familiar with all pedagogical literature, which she recommends to director and teachers at appropriate times.

The cabinet arranges seminars for teachers on such subjects as "what is new"; "development of speech"; "counting in math"; "drawing"; "nature"; and "play."

The kindergartens themselves often form groups (*kusts*) to investigate some phase of kindergarten work. Each *kust* is led by a young director, or an experienced teacher, who invites teachers from four or five other kindergartens located nearby in the same region, to join in an investigation of some particular question of interest, such as the physical-training program or the art program.

If physical training is the chosen topic, one school volunteers to study a particular phase of physical training, such as the children's walks, while another investigates the development of movement in the child, and a third reports on active play and sports. The results of the investigation are presented in a symposium at one of the kindergartens and all of the teachers from the region are invited to a collective viewing and discussion. At the end of the year all the regions in a town compile a handbook of information on the year's progress.

The Department of Foreign Teaching Theory and Practice of the Academy of Pedagogical Sciences prepares news bulletins and abstracts of interesting foreign education books and articles, and these are sent to every teacher-training college, refresher course, and education office in the Soviet Union.

A Siberian schoolteacher will get a full translation of an important article on American education soon after it comes out in the United States. Soviet educators, familiar with translations of Montessori, Dewey, Kilpatrick and Thorndike from the past, now know such modern books as Jerome Bruner's *The Process of Education,* Fritz Machlup's *The Production and Distribution of Knowledge in the United States,* and more recently, translations of Dr. Spock. Soviet translators were familiar with the works of the Swiss psychologist Piaget, before Piaget had translations of Soviet works.

The K. D. Ushinsky State Scientific Library of Public Education, in Moscow, receives more than eighty educational journals from the United States alone, in addition to books and pamphlets from the United States and the rest of the world. Every year groups of Soviet educators visit the United States and other foreign countries and foreign educators visit the Soviet Union.

Even more important are the visits of parents and grandparents to the schools. Some Communists at various times have suggested that children be reared in boarding schools, away from the distracting influence of parents, but today the parent's influence is considered too valuable to be eliminated. Today's parents are specifically trained to work with the school.

"Simply to give life to man is not enough," parents are told. "You must make this life good, bright and useful to society. In this is the duty of parents."

The major link between home and school is the Parents' Committee, which operates under the director of the kindergarten. These parents have contact with the pedagogical collective, know many of the children and most of the families in the neighborhood.

The school also advises the children's parents to teach the children to lay out their school clothes the night before, to see that their shoes are shined before going to bed and to check other items listed in the school's "sanitary notebook," such as hair and nails, and pocket handkerchiefs.

The school stresses that the parents must "listen to" the child when he comes home from school, as this not only is important to his development, but also will bring parent and child closer together.

The Parents' Committee chooses a presidium, which organizes the work of its committees. Each member of the presidium is attached to one of the commissions of the committee, such as the "Educational Commission," the "Commission for Mass Culture," or "Pedagogical Propaganda." There are also commissions for sanitation, household affairs, observations of socially useful labor, and conversations with prominent local civic leaders. The actual problems of each commission are worked out on the basis of past experience and present goals, in conversation between the school director and the leader of the presidium.

The Parents' Committee advises tact in handling parents wherever possible. The chairman of the educational commission advises the members of his committee on the best methods possible of dealing with parents. In one school the committee decided to visit the families of children who were doing badly in school and talk to them in friendly fashion about the children's needs. When the committee members did this tactfully, good results were obtained. Otherwise they only succeeded in antagonizing the parents.

The mass-culture commission organizes lectures for parents, plans group excursions, holidays, and "evenings" of lectures and discussions. Specialists from various fields of science and art are brought to the school, where they show the children some of their work, and tell them about their careers. They also help the children with various projects. The mass-culture commission also organizes exhibitions of children's art, and plans sightseeing trips around town or to the country in summer.

The commission for pedagogical propaganda organizes lectures on such themes as "personal example and authority of parents"; "training the child's will"; "how to help children to learn better"; "physical education of the child in the family"; and "moral and work training in the family." This committee also meets regularly to discuss books and magazine articles, which they recommend for parents' reading.

The sanitary commission looks after the sanitary conditions of the school and courtyard.

Parents who do not fulfill their home duties to the child are asked to come to the school with the child and discuss the problem with the Parents' Committee. Suggestions are given, and if parents ignore the suggestions, the Parents' Committe has a powerful weapon not available to most American P.T.A.'s. A parent who does not heed a committee warning may find himself "posted" on the wall newspaper of his factory or other place of employment. When fellow workers read that Ivan Ivanov is not fulfilling his parental duties and that Ivan junior is doing poorly in Kindergarten No. 908, they put pressure on Ivan senior to straighten the matter out before the honor of the factory is blackened.

·IV·

The Making of Soviet Citizens

BUILDING A NEW Communist society is a task for everyone, and for the new society a new man is needed who combines, as the Soviets say, "spiritual wealth, moral purity and physical perfection." The ideal evolved slowly after 1917, when mere existence was a struggle. One of Lenin's first goals after the Revolution was to eliminate illiteracy. He and his wife, Nadezhda Krupskaya, were very much interested in education. Krupskaya (she is never called Mrs. Lenin) was particularly interested in preschool education, and was familiar with the work of Montessori and Froebel as well as kindergarten practice in France, England and other European countries that she and Lenin visited during their years of exile. She was particularly impressed with the work of the prerevolutionary educator K. D. Ushinsky (1824–1870).

Russia, Ushinsky felt, was distinguished from all other countries by its language and its poetry created by the simple people. Thus, he thought, Russian education should be national in character. He believed that each country had its own notion of the ideal man, conditioned by its own national culture and environment. He noted that people were educated by their native language long before there were books and schools, and that "the child who does not master his native tongue becomes an adult who does not understand his native country." Ushinsky also believed that the first year of a child's life establishes what will later become his second nature, and Krupskaya agreed.

Even before the Revolution, Krupskaya had advocated the establishment of institutions to care for the children of working mothers, so it was natural that preschool education was included in the first system of popular education drawn up immediately after the Revolution. However, there was little money for any school, and when Lenin's Education Minister Lunacharsky said that the number of pupils in the elementary schools was falling off due to lack of funds, Lenin urged a cut in naval expenditures—"We don't need a fleet, but an increase in the expenditure on schools is desperately needed."

From her observations Krupskaya concluded that in capitalistic countries rich people did not send their children to kindergarten, feeling that kindergartens were for poor people and the children of workers. The Marxist idea of the social education of children through a system of socialized preschool institutions particularly interested her. The preschool institutions, she felt, would serve the dual purpose of freeing the mother for work and giving a child useful knowledge and pleasure as well. The child would be met at school with smiles and conversation, and assigned to some group; each group would have its own activity, such as digging in the earth, watering plants, washing dishes, sewing, drawing, reading, singing, or simply playing.

Krupskaya devoted a great deal of her time to educational matters, both during Lenin's lifetime and after his death. In 1969 the whole Soviet Union celebrated the hundredth anniversary of her birth, and every kindergarten had a Krupskaya corner with pictures and stories of her life, particularly her life for and with little school children. Krupskaya's influence is particularly strong in the field of preschool education. She and Anton Semyonovich Makarenko (1888–1939; he died the same year Krupskaya did) are the most-quoted Soviet educators.

After the Revolution thousands of children, made homeless by the World War, civil war and famine, roamed through Russia. These bands of wild children lived by pillaging and attacking the inhabitants of the countryside. The authorities were unable to cope with them. In 1920 the Department of Public Education authorized Makarenko to set up a school for these *bezprizornyi,* the word for "homeless," but translated by most people as "delinquent." Makarenko himself believed there were no bad children, only bad methods of education.

Makarenko described his experiences with the *bezprizornyi* in

The Road to Life, which, with his *Learning to Live,* his *Problems of Communist Education* and his *Book for Parents,* expounded a philosophy of education still practiced today. Makarenko tells how he surmounted the problems which arose—stealing, gambling, drinking, lice. Gradually, through the hungry days of the famine of 1921 and 1922, Makarenko's colony of *bezprizornyi* became a collective commune run by the children themselves.

Work, which had been undertaken at first as a basic requirement for existence, soon became one of the keystones of Makarenko's method. His experience with the first colony, known as the Gorky Colony, convinced him that the most powerful educative force was socially useful labor. It was through labor that the Colony became a real collective, and when he started a new commune, named for Felix Dzerzhinsky, the accent was again on productive labor, not just for economic ends but as a means of character building.

Any educator, Makarenko thought, must know exactly what he wanted to create—"But if you are to be responsible for your production you must know at every step in your life as a teacher what you want and how you are going to get it."

These goals do not remain immutable, Makarenko said, but change as society changes, the aims of education arising from the social needs of each society. Makarenko was convinced that the traits of the Soviet personality differed from the traits of the bourgeois personality and that this necessarily entailed a different form of education. He believed that the bourgeois state, educating the child for the individual struggle for existence, had to stress "cunning, diplomacy, fighting one's own personal battles, fighting for oneself."

The bourgeois dependence on power and position were to be replaced in Soviet society by a dependency of mutual respect and cooperation. The common aims of the collective determine the private aims of the members of the collective. Makarenko did not think this was an easy goal. It had many complex ramifications: "And only where the common and the personal aims coincide and there is no disharmony whatever, only that collective can be called a Soviet collective."

The primary collective must never shut itself off from the rest of society. The children of the collective should always regard themselves as part of Soviet society. Makarenko thought that the children in his colonies were "first and foremost, citizens of their country. And that is the principal difference between our children and those of any other society in the world."

Makarenko wanted the school to be a single collective, and he disapproved of the practice of so-called normal children with normal homes who had one collective in school, another with the Pioneers (a youth organization analogous to the Boy Scouts) and still another at summer camp. He believed that there should be a single direction to the child's goals and education.

Makarenko relied on tradition to cement the collective. Among Makarenko's traditions were early-morning roll call in which the duty officer taking the roll call had the right to impose punishment. Another tradition along the same line was for a young girl to be on duty every day to enforce sanitation regulations. This girl, with a red-cross band on her arm, could order anyone to leave the table to wash his hands or reprimand anyone for being dirty or having dirty quarters.

Esteem for the flag was another tradition. General meetings were always opened by bugles to call people to the meeting, then the orchestra played three marches. When the music stopped, Makarenko would say, "Attention, the flag!" Everyone stood up and the flag-bearers marched in to a special flag salute by the orchestra. The flag-bearers themselves had special privileges. They could not be punished or addressed familiarly while they were guarding the flag. On trips, someone was always on duty to guard the flag. Makarenko's critics argued that it was silly for some boy to sit up all night with the flag, losing sleep and ruining his health, but Makarenko was adamant. It was a tradition.

Even when the colony was very poor, Makarenko used part of his allotment to build a greenhouse in which to grow flowers, and bowls of fresh flowers were placed in the children's dormitories. There was never an oilcloth cover on the dining table but always a white cloth. Makarenko contended that neatness could never be taught if spills could be so easily wiped up.

These traditions were all part of what Makarenko called the

"principle of perspectives: to educate a man is to furnish him with a perspective leading to the morrow's joy." Style and tone were the outward forms of this striving toward the future. As a practical proposition, Makarenko found that a collective that is well dressed is much easier to manage.

Children must have a sense of the confidence in their own worth. They were taught to be polite, not to slouch, and to be considerate of others. Makarenko felt that these outward forms helped the child put inward brakes on his behavior.

"The ideas of Krupskaya and Makarenko formed the foundation on which we have built our system of preschool education," Dr. A. V. Zaporozhets told us on our third visit to the Soviet Union in 1967.

Dr. Zaporozhets was a pleasant, intelligent man who spoke perfect English and was completely familiar with preschool education in the United States as well as in the rest of the world.

"The aim of *yasli* and *detsky sad*," Dr. Zaporozhets said, "is to help the mother contribute to the cultural and political work of the country, and to give the child a multisided development— physical, moral and mental. There are both social and pedagogical aims. We have created the most humane and democratic system in the world for the education of little children. Our system is based on the tremendous potentialities of development of each child and the strengthening of these individual potentialities through education under social conditions of life."

Dr. Zaporozhets told us that the 1962 *Program of Instruction in the Kindergarten* was a milestone in its approach to preschool education, although both Krupskaya and Makarenko had recognized the importance of early education, Makarenko believing that ninety percent of the educational process took place before the child was five. The 1962 *Program,* with its 1965 revision, was the first complete guide to the life of the child from babyhood to enrollment in school, Dr. Zaporozhets said.

"But" he said, shaking his head, "time does not stand still. The Soviet family has reached higher cultural and material levels, and the Soviet child now is bigger, smarter and healthier. He is able to solve more complicated problems than the people of my generation could at his age. We are about to shorten the primary grades from four years to three, and this puts more demands on the kindergarten. We need a new program to keep up with Soviet progress toward Communism, so the Preschool Institute, the Institute of Psychology and the Institute of General and Polytechnical Education of the Academy of Pedagogical Sciences are working with cadres of the pedagogical institutes to create a new, improved program, which should go into effect in 1969."

Dr. Zaporozhets explained that investigations had already shown that the potential for development of the preschool child was much greater than anyone had previously thought possible. "Even in problems of character," he said, "the impulsive, involuntary behavior that was considered so typical of little children, can be overcome by education. The children can learn to govern their own conduct and establish norms of moral conduct."

"You are interested in moral development at this early age?" my husband asked.

"Very much so," Dr. Zaporozhets answered. "Some of your American educators think it is impossible for these very young children to understand moral norms, but we believe it is possible. There are many factors involved, and it is easier to teach the child to read or to count, but it is important to form an adequate moral notion of upbringing so that the child understands what is good or bad in his own behavior.

"The child is primitive, but he can understand. The idea is to give him a real understanding of moral behavior so that he does not simply form mechanical habits. He is egocentric at this age, but he must have moral action."

As Dr. Zaporozhets spoke, I was thinking of Dr. Spock's *Common Sense Book of Baby and Child Care,* the Bible of American child rearing, which claims that Americans have lost their old-fashioned convictions about the kind of morals and character they want their children to have. Dr. Spock says that Americans have even lost their convictions about the purpose of human existence, that America is a child-centered country, where children are free to set their own aims, too often based on materialistic

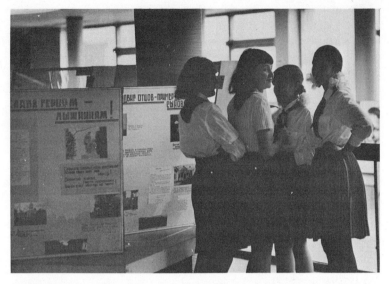

Young Pioneers in a Pioneer Palace. The activities of these Russian equivalents of Girl Scouts emphasize good peer relations.

values. Dr. Spock's plea for a return to old-fashioned morality and idealism sounded almost like the Soviet goal, as Dr. Zaporozhets outlined it.

"Don't all people really want the same thing for their children?" I wondered. "How do we achieve this goal?"

"Children's society must be organized," Dr. Zaporozhets said. "In Soviet education the child has practical moral experience through collective activities. Good relations among the children themselves in the peer group are as important as the relations between the teacher and the child."

Dr. Zaporozhets explained some of the research done by his Institute—Usova's investigation of play as a form of organization of a child's life; Nechaeva's studies of the interrelations of children in their activities; and Markova's on perfecting the program to form the desired qualities of mutual assistance and high morality as well as to improve the child's mental and physical abilities.

"Montessori thought that the child under six had no sense of right or wrong," Dr. Zaporozhets said, "and that it was only in the period from six to twelve that the child began to be conscious of right and wrong." Piaget, too, considered the young child egocentric and too young for moral judgments."

Dr. Zaporozhets said that some foreign educators felt that the child could be taught to read at the age of two, whereas Piaget felt that the child was incapable of reaching the stage of development at which he could read until later.

"We think that education plays a leading role in the child's development and that today we can achieve results unheard of in the past, but we want all-around development of the child. We think each stage must be built on the foundation of the preceding stage. The stages are not isolated phases in the child's life. They must be connected. Experiments of Leontev, Galperin and Elkonin show that the educational process must be organized under social conditions. Without social conditions a human being cannot develop properly. The activity of the child himself is one of the most important factors in the development; but this must be guided by education, as spontaneous experience is too slow. Social education in the Soviet Union means experience in the collective, but it must be a true collective and not just a group of children without any inner connection."

He explained that the child must become acquainted with his surroundings and that this cognition of the environment begins with sensation and perception.

"It is essential to form the child's sensory abilities in the early years. Usova found that sensory perception occurs not by formal exercises of the sense organs as in Montessori—buttoning boards or other isolated practice boards—but in the process of intelligent activity in everyday occupations, such as actually buttoning up your own jacket. We also believe that these processes can be taught," Dr. Zaporozhets explained that both Piaget and Montessori felt that learning occurred in stages and that a child could not be pushed too far beyond his normal stage, whereas the Soviets believed that all stages of development could be speeded by instruction. Montessori wanted the child to discover things through his own unaided investigation, while the Soviets wanted to avoid time-consuming methods of trial and error and thus emphasized learning through direct instruction.

We were shown a picture of a child guiding a toy car through a maze and were told that the child who made preliminary investigatory motions of feeling the maze with his hands before guiding the car through the maze, made fewer mistakes than the child who had not had the preliminary tactile investigation.

"The orienting movements in the young child are naturally very imperfect, but with instruction the achievement level is greatly improved. We feel, unlike Piaget, that these processes of perception can be taught. Our Institute studies the connection between instruction and natural development. We want to teach the child to think, so we are studying the thought processes and how to perfect elementary mental operations, how to arouse the child's curiosity and his wish to learn. Children learn through activities with specific objects, in play as well as in classroom studies."

Dr. Zaporozhets explained the active nature of the processes of perception. Visual perception involves orienting eye movements, tactile perception involves the active feeling process. Soviet babies are encouraged to investigate an object through all their senses and are shown how to look at something, how to investigate a new object with the fingers to determine its form and weight. These investigations are strengthened with the use of words.

"In other countries, educators have found that it is possible to teach the child to read and write and do arithmetic, at six, or even five, years of age," Dr. Zaporozhets continued. He handed me a copy of the new 1967 *Handbook,* pointing to the first pages, where I read:

"To provide a happy childhood for every child is one of the most important and noble tasks in the building of a Communist society."

·V·

Everything Begins with Play

On our fourth trip to the Soviet Union in 1969, we again visited the Scientific Research Institute of Preschool Education, this time for more detailed information. I found that most of the top authorities were gathered together in the Preschool Institute. It was as though Jerome Bruner, Dr. Spock, Haim Ginott, Gesell, the American authorities on Montessori and Piaget, and other famous American educators were united in a small government agency in Washington, D.C. The Washington agency would have been housed in a splendid marble building, whereas the Preschool Institute is in a shabby old building with worn stairs leading to offices on the second floor.

The Institute conducts research on preschool education and uses several Moscow *kombinat*s as models for investigation and experimentation.

On the basis of the Institute's research the *Program* is drawn up. The new 1969 *Program* stresses development of the child's powers of observation, curiosity, ability to think and to speak. The child must be aware of inner connections of the world around him as well as the external names of the objects which surround him.

For the nursery-school and kindergarten child the most important learning comes through play, and all the departments of the Institute are interested in the process. Role and subject play involve moral norms, active play concerns the lab of physical education, building play and didactic play require a study of the child's mental abilities, and there are musical games and picture games which concern the lab specializing in aesthetic education.

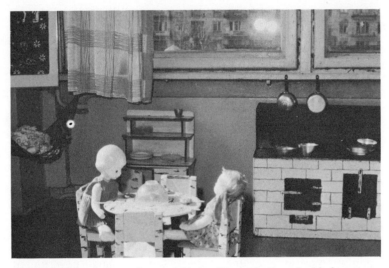

Toys duplicate various phases of Soviet life, including the kitchen stove.

Play involves the total child. The members of the Institute believe that the earlier the child learns to play, the sooner he learns independence in his activities, which is one of the main goals for the child.

The members of the Institute all agreed that early childhood was the most important period for the development of the personality. How this personality is formed was considered a more complicated matter.

A researcher from the psychological lab talked about the Bridge School, in Boston, which she had visited; she said that she disapproved of the system of permissive education in the United States, where the child does what he wants to instead of what he should do.

"We think it is important to learn systematically," Madame Repina said. "It's not conformist education. We don't hold the child tight, but we do want him to be a responsible member of the collective. In our psychology department we try to find out how the child feels about the collective, where he learns social relations. Social aims are very important. The children themselves have a profound effect on the other children in the collective."

The psychology department, she said, was concerned with the development of the child's ability and the diagnosis of his problems. She was interested in the way the child uses sensory perception to investigate something new. He begins to classify an object visually, tactually and otherwise, and the psychologists are trying to find just what processes go on in the child's mind at this stage. How does he choose the method by which he investigates a new object? Can these methods be taught?

On the whole, the Soviets disapprove of tests which classify children as bright or stupid by the time they are in first grade. They have studied the work of Binet, Snyder and other testers, and they see the need for diagnostic work, but they are inclined to believe with their scientist Vygotsky that the best test for intelligence is the way a child responds to instruction.

We were surprised to find many of the leaders in education still working with vitality and enthusiasm after a half century in Soviet education. Madame V. G. Nechaeva, with pale-reddish hair and a sweet, spiritual face, has been concerned with the moral nature of the child since early Revolutionary days, and Madame E. I. Radina, of the psychology lab, was said to have worked here before the Revolution. These people have survived the many changes of Party policy in the past fifty years and give a continuity to Soviet educational development.

In investigating the thought patterns of the very young child, the laboratory studies the way a child adapts himself to the world of objects which surround him. The Soviets do not believe that the child is born with a ready-made ability to think. This ability is developed in a series of social contacts in which the child is instructed by society, for society. The child comes into the world from the beginning not just as a spectator but as a participant, although the adults of the world, consciously or unconsciously, try to make the child like themselves.

One of the experiments in Radina's laboratory attempted to discover the way a child uses the objects around him. When the child is only six months old he is knocking two objects together to produce a sound and perhaps a month later, he is using one object as a tool to move another object.

He has learned about other tools—the spoon with which he is fed, the shovel with which he digs in the sandbox. He sees people using hammers, spading the garden, and occupied with other tools. Soviet psychologists think that the use of tools (and language is considered a tool) and the act of thinking are closely connected.

In an experiment wherein children between the ages of eleven months and two and a half years were used, one child would sit at a table, whose top came up to his arm pits. On the table was a toy, just out of reach, and a stick which was easily accessible. The experimenter asked the child to get the toy, and the child would stretch his arm across the table top, reaching for it. The one-and-a-half-year-olds trying to reach the toy, often appealed to the experimenter, "*Dai* [Give]." Younger children, unable to reach the toy, simply stretched silently toward the unattainable toy. Sometimes the children tried to reach the toy in a round-about fashion, by getting up from their chairs and walking around to the other side of the table, but were told, "Sit in your chair!"

Next the child's attention was attracted to the stick. He began to investigate and discovered the possibility of using the stick as a means of reaching the toy he wanted, making the mental connection of "means—goal." Some sticks have rings on the ends of them which hook on various toys and the child becomes very interested in the way he can move things with the stick, pushing and pulling the toy in various ways.

Similar experiments have been tried with chimpanzees (in other countries as well as in Russia), and the chimpanzee also uses the stick to get the object he wants; but in the Soviet view, the difference between the chimp and the child is that the chimp, achieving his end, forgets the tool, while the tool itself continues to fascinate the child. Moreover, the child can achieve the desired result in three or four attempts, whereas it takes the chimp about twenty-five tries.

Soviet educators believe in giving very little children concrete problems to solve. They think that by solving problems the child builds experience in thinking, strengthens motor habits, and gains sensory knowledge, all of which form the basis of elementary work operations. As he learns to solve simple problems he is given more complicated ones (using the stick to get a toy out of a bottle or putting rings on a stick) with the hope that he will use his knowledge now in his independent play as well as in his lessons.

Radina showed us a simple little tower of colored rings on a stick—the rings come off the stick and the problem is to put them back on in the correct order so that they form a smooth pyramid. A teacher or nurse shows the child how to take the rings off and put them back on, and then the child is asked to do it himself. Properly, Radina said, "the child should line the rings flat on the table in the right order before attempting to put them on the stick."

In every *yasli* we visited, at least one child was manipulating a similar toy. We saw a number of babies who could not walk taking the rings off the stick. This serious-looking business is also called play, the "poetry" of the child's life. Play is the very life of the child, Makarenko thought—and by play he meant something more than just playing football or some other game. He meant that the child "plays a little every minute of his life, he soars a bit in his imagination, makes tiny flights of fancy, he acts a little, and in play feels rather bigger than he is."

The baby's first toy (after his thumb) is the mobile of beads, butterflies or balls hung over his crib while he is still in the hospital and again over his bed at home. A nurse or midwife has already checked his home to see that his bath utensils are separate from the cooking utensils, that his bed is metal, washed in disinfectant and that his baby carriage, bought at Children's World for about forty dollars, is also sanitary and easily washable.

The mothers are reassured when the doctor at the Polyclinic tells them the baby must be a month or a month and a half old before he can hold his head up even for a few seconds and that most of his first actions are due to unconditioned reflexes. The pupils of his eyes narrow in response to light, a touch on the sole of his foot causes him to spread his toes wide and a touch on the hand brings an instant grasping reaction.

Physical training and play are interwoven in the preschool years, particularly for the younger members of the *yasli,* who begin their formal exercises as soon as they enter, sometimes as early as two months of age. Exercising the babies was the favorite activity in most of the schools we visited.

The director and the other people who showed us around always displayed a certain anticipatory excitement just before we reached the room where the youngest children were playing. "Now we come to the best part," they would say, seating us beside a table.

When a nurse brought in a young baby, the one- and two-year-olds looked up from their toys or toddled over to the table to watch. The nurse placed the baby on the table, which was covered with pads and a sheet. When the baby was undressed he turned his head to us and smiled through three fingers stuck in his mouth. The nurse, making cooing noises, massaged the naked baby's arms and legs, then flipped him deftly over on his stomach as she massaged his spine. Again he was turned on his back, his stomach massaged, his legs raised and lowered, the soles of his feet gently bent, his legs folded to his chest, then his arms crossed over his chest, and finally he was pulled to a sitting position. The one- and two-year-olds usually seemed more serious than the baby, and their smiles were less frequent, their faces showing an intense effort to understand what was going on.

"Do you want to see how we teach them to crawl?" we were asked in one nursery. "We like them to crawl before they sit, as this leads to more activity, but some children crawl first and others sit before they crawl. The development of the nervous system controls these movements, which are also influenced by the development of the child's organs of sight, sound and feeling."

After the baby had had his exercises the nurse gave him a ball, then turned him gently over on his stomach as he held on to the ball. She put the ball just out of his reach as he was lying on his back but in such a position that he could see it. His fingers twitched as though holding the ball, as he reached out

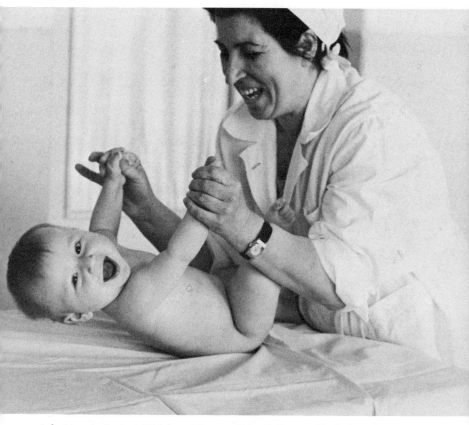

A happy student at Kishinev Nursery School No. 5. He is learning to exercise in response to the rhythm hummed by his teacher.

for it, turning onto his stomach and finally crawling toward the ball.

"We build up a reflex of turning over on the stomach when holding the ball," the teacher said, "so he associates the stomach position with holding the ball. Now when he wants to get hold of the ball he automatically turns on his stomach and starts to reach. We put the ball a little farther away each time, so he has to crawl toward it. He crawls without realizing it at first, but

A parrot's tail just fits a baby's mouth. "Taste is one method of investigating a new object," says a teacher.

soon it becomes a conditioned reflex which he can do at will. He not only has learned to crawl but is learning to think."

Play is a serious business for the first few years and seems to consist more of putting toys in the mouth than of handling them. The smaller babies are put in individual cribs, which look like large basketball nets, or in group playpens, which may hold five or ten children. They stand, if they are able, holding on to the slats of their crib, looking out reflectively while they chew the end of a celluloid parrot, whose tail seems particularly made for babies' mouths.

"Taste is one method of investigating a new object," a teacher says calmly, watching as one child after putting the parrot in his mouth throws it outside the playpen. "A parent should never punish a child for behavior that is typical for his age." She picked up the parrot and handed it back to the child, who went through the same routine with the toy from mouth to floor. "If the child is destructive with his toys later on, it is probably because he does not understand the rules of the game. "At this age, the child is behaving normally."

The nursery children were the only ones who seemed upset when strangers came into their rooms, and usually one or two of the children would cry when we came in with a group of educators. The nurses comforted them but did not act alarmed, and usually the children accepted us after a few minutes.

Another child cried at first then set off resolutely toward a sliding board in one corner of the playroom. The slide had some low steps leading to the top, and the child went up the steps easily, his attention directed more at us than at the steps. At the top he took another stride without looking where he was going and stepped off onto the vertical slide unexpectedly. He went down with such a bump that we and the director were about to cry out and rush to help him, when the nurse shook her head at us.

The child picked himself up, looked around to see whether or not he should cry, decided against it, and started back up the slide. This time he held on to the railing of the stairs as he climbed the steps, and at the top carefully lowered himself to the slide before he let go the railing. At the bottom, the look of triumph on his face was equaled only by the one on the nurse's face.

In another nursery, we watched the children as they practiced walking. The teacher had placed a board on the floor, and the children tried to walk on it without stepping on the floor. When they could walk on the board they began to walk on a log placed a few inches above the floor. Then they practiced walking on different surfaces—grass, cement, smooth surfaces, and rough and hilly ground. As they improved, the obstacles became more complicated—ditches to jump across, hoops to crawl through. They were taught to step backward, to jump forward, to circle slowly in place, and they seemed to be enjoying all the exercises immensely, spurred on by the desire to learn to walk well enough to go on the regular walks the older children take.

At a year and a half to two years the child is ready for a walk, though it may not last more than five or ten minutes at first. Then the walk is lengthened to fifteen minutes, with a rest of not less than ten minutes afterward. At two or three years of age the children are taking twenty- to thirty-minute walks, and when they get older they will have three walks a day, in the morning, after *poldnik* (afternoon snack) and after supper.

The child of a year and a half should be able to climb a stepladder, climb over a log, climb under a bench and crawl through a hoop. He can roll a ball, throw it to another child, bounce it up and down, and throw it in a specified direction. He has enough control of his movements so that he can do a simple dance. He may even feel he is too old for the first games he learned in his crib, though he enjoys seeing his mother or teacher play *ladushki* (like pat-a-cake) and *soroka-belobaka* (a game that involves tickling) with a smaller child.

By the time he is two he is very lively and does not stay in one place for more than a few minutes at a time, even though he walks, swaying from side to side, his hands pressed to his body or one hand out, lightly waving, his walking a series of flat-footed falls forward.

Whether the two-year-old child's life is chaotic or organized, A. P. Usova felt, depends upon education. She did not agree with Western educators who felt that the child must learn from trial and error, but felt guidance could help the child avoid time-consuming errors. Even a two-year-old could learn to look and listen and to actively imitate the actions of a grown person.

E. I. Radina, who is in charge of the Department of Early Age in the Preschool Institute, showed us some of the toys she used for children three years old and under. In addition to the well-known blocks and rings on sticks, there is the Russian hollow wooden doll, Matreshka, which comes apart into two pieces. Inside is a smaller Matreshka, and when that doll is opened, there is still a smaller doll inside that one. Occasionally there will be a fourth doll inside the third, but there are always at least three.

When Radina gave children toys that were new to them they used them in various ways. Unless an adult or an older child showed them how to open Matreshka, the child played with her like an ordinary doll. Upon instruction, 95.5 percent followed the directions of the teacher. Only 4.5 percent could not follow the in-

A sense of balance is considered very important (above). Physical education with particular emphasis on coordination is stressed in all preschool programs in the Soviet Union. A child should be able to crawl through a hoop (right).

structions or disregarded them and continued to play with the doll in the way they wished. When the use of the toys was interesting to the children they were anxious to learn the next step, thus creating a "learning readiness," which seemed important. Individual instruction also gave quicker results than group instruction. In groups the children imitated each other, and the influence of the children on each other was strong. Many of the children listened to and watched the teacher's explanation, and then looked around to see what the other children were doing before they started work.

When the children were not shown how to do something, they often just knocked the pieces of blocks together or put them in their mouths, showing no inclination to do what the teacher suggested. Some tasks that were presented demanded only mechanical imitation, while others demanded actual thought by the child. The young child will imitate hand clapping or obey a command to hand someone the "large ball" or the "small ring" almost without reflection. With a more difficult task like making a chair and a table out of blocks, the child does better if the adult asks a leading question like, "The doll sits in the chair, but the little cup sits on the table. Where is the table?" The child's performance improves when he has to think.

Since two- and three-year-old children are so active physically the Soviets include some element of movement in all didactic play. As the child is most active in the morning, this is the time chosen for most active play periods. The child under two has had individual exercises, but at two he begins daily group exercises. If the weather permits, the exercises are done outdoors. If indoors, they are done before open windows, as the Soviet people must have fresh air.

The goals of physical exercises and active play are coordination, speed and confidence. The child plays native Russian games like "Here Comes the Horned Goat," or "Mishka Walks in the Field," as well as "Drop the Handkerchief," "Hide and Seek," and team games. Games such as "Bees in the Beehive" show the Russian love of nature. In this game the children follow the queen bee, winding into a tight spiral. "*Bzz, bzz, bzz,* bees in the beehive," the children sing, until suddenly the queen shouts, "*Medved!* [Bear!]," and everyone runs back to the beehive.

Another favorite is "Cat," in which the children stand in a circle holding hands, then dance and sing a song about a cat.

The cat comes up and asks if there is a mouse anywhere around. "No," the children answer, "she has gone to get us some salt meat." The children do another dance, and the cat comes back to ask about the mouse again. "Here she is," the children say. "Catch her so she won't go out again." If the cat can't catch the mouse, the teacher should, according to Russian textbooks on play, "tactfully interrupt the game and relieve the running children."

Exercises for the two-and-a-half-to-three-year-old child are imaginative as well as vigorous. We saw the children lie on the floor and make their legs revolve violently in the air in imitation of a velocipede, and jump around the room with both feet together in imitation of a sparrow. Before long we became expert enough to distinguish the arm waving that represented a butterfly from the arm waving that represented a bird. The Russians were more observant about nature than we were, so such fine distinctions were lost on us at first. Children go to the forests, learn to pick mushrooms (a favorite Russian pastime) and learn the name of the trees in the forest. In the game "Find This Tree" the children are given a leaf and told to find the tree it matches.

One expert on play said that while it might seem that children had mastered the art of movement already, since they can walk, run, jump, and make sudden, unexpected movements, these movements are really incomplete and lacking in deftness and coordinated skill. Less active children, under the influence of play, are helped to move and speak as they never would outside of play.

When the teacher sees that the games have become too easy for the children, more complicated games are substituted, because the child must never be bored by play. If the teacher finds the children are not getting along well with a certain game, she must discover why the game is not going well. Has she explained the rules of the game fully? Are the children tired, or sick? Are the children happy in the collective? Has the teacher convinced the children that they must fulfill their task?

When certain basic skills have been developed, the children

Even play is a learning experience, helping to develop basic coordinated skills. (Below) Passing a rubber ball in a relay game up and down the line stresses both physical coordination and group activity and introduces competition between teams as well.

(Above) Games involving singing are favorites with the children, and they help develop coordination. (Below) At very early stages the children are encouraged to participate in role play, frequently involving family units. These children are mamas and papas looking out for their children.

may start sports. Just as I had to practice tennis on the back-board before going onto the tennis court, so the children must learn various fundamentals before taking up a sport.

The first ski lesson is given when the child is three and con-sists of learning to put on and take off the skis, followed by walking on skis on level ground without a ski pole. Next, the children learn to turn in place, making a "fan" in the snow. The children are very proud of the fan pattern in the snow. As a reward for a good fan they are allowed to use the ski poles, and before long they are skiing in the parks, and later they try to find out who is fastest on skis, though competition is not used with the younger children.

Ice-skating instruction begins in similar fashion at age five. The children first learn to put on and take off the ice skates. When the children first stand up on skates they hold on to some-thing, but they are also instructed on how to test the ice, how to keep from interfering with one another and how to fall for-ward or to the side, and not backward, which is more dangerous. The first lesson lasts no more than ten minutes, then the lessons are lengthened, until the child is skating for thirty to thirty-five minutes with two recesses of two or three minutes each.

Table tennis is taken up with even more care, starting with exercises in handling the paddle, lessons in bouncing the ball, and exercises to strengthen specific muscles, as well as instruc-tion in the rules of the game. Swimming is also carefully taught.

We saw about two thousand Soviet children under seven years of age, and we were particularly impressed with the interest the children showed in what they were doing. Our visits were only momentary distractions in the child's day and did not really take their concentration from the business at hand, whether it was playing, painting or doing arithmetic. On visits to American kindergartens we saw much more boredom as well as more obstreperous behavior, and I think the difference is in the thor-oughness of preparation shown by the Soviets.

The Soviet *yasli* and *detsky sad* expect the child to perform to the limit of his ability, but they know what his span of atten-tion is. They have found that even the older groups get restless and stop paying attention after fifteen to twenty minutes of one activity; so listening endurance is built up gradually, as in a physical-fitness program. The Soviets believe that self-control can be taught; so they teach it in an orderly fashion. The child whose muscles have been trained for a certain game, is going to play it better than a child who is uncoordinated. The uncoordinated child, feeling his failure, not only gives up the game but has harmed his psyche with his feelings of failure. The Soviets try to keep the child's interest at a high level and his feelings of failure to a minimum, and they do seem to have succeeded very well with the preschoolers.

The Soviets readily admit that there is no sure recipe for conditioning the child, but they do feel that certain principles are involved. According to Pavlov's theories of conditioned reflexes, each undesirable (or desirable) form of conduct is a system of fixed reflexes. However, the mother or teacher may become a "switching agent" to change this habit. The old habit, if not strengthened will die out. The new habit must have sufficiently strong reinforcement; and finally, the new system of fixed reflexes must be strengthened in a peaceful atmosphere, with a sound emotional background.

The principal theme at the Fiftieth Anniversary Conference of Preschool Workers was the education of children through play, and particular interest was expressed in how to handle arguments between children in the course of play.

Soviet psychologists and educators are fascinated with the behavior of little children, both for its intrinsic interest and as a basis for molding a new man. They like to analyze the child's behavior, but they also seem amazed at the remarkable mechanism of childhood. In one experiment they observed some children playing house.

Ira, five years and two months old, expressed the wish to play the role of "Mama"; and Olya, five years and six months of age, agreed to be the daughter. Both girls had dolls, or "children," which they put to bed. Then the girls sat down on chairs and were silent for a while.

The experimenter started the conversation. "Are your children sick? We'll have to call the doctor. Who will be the doctor?"

Olya: "Looba will be the doctor. Looba, come here, you will be the doctor." Looba came over to the girls and waited for another cue, but Ira brushed him aside.

Ira: "I'll cure them myself. I'm just now giving them medicine."

She took a cup and spoon and brought medicine to the lips of the dolls. Then in a "mother's" voice she said, "You have to, you have to drink it."

Since Looba had not been able to enter the game, he left. Olya tried to take one of the dolls in her arms, but Ira objected.

Ira: "That's not necessary. Don't do that."

Olya: "Let me. I'll take her in my arms."

Ira: "No, let her lie here. She has to lie down."

Olya put the doll down, agreeing with Ira. The girls sat silently for a while, evidently not knowing in what form to develop the subject further.

Ira: "And here's our dog. She's lying on the floor. I must cover her up."

Olya: "You don't have to cover her up. What are you thinking of?"

Ira: "No, we have to or she'll catch cold."

Olya: "You don't cover up dogs."

Ira: "No, you do cover them up. I'm the mama. I know best."

Ira proceeded to cover the toy dog. Olya again tried to take her "daughter" in her arms. Ira immediately left the dog.

Ira: "I told you—it's not necessary to take her in your arms."

Olya: "She's sick. You take sick children in your arms."

Ira: "Let her lie there, or I won't play."

Olya gave in. Kolya, who had been watching, came up to the girls.

Experimenter: "Girls, here comes Kolya. He will be the papa."

Kolya showed a readiness to enter the game, but not knowing what to do, he waited.

Olya: "He's still at work. The papa still hasn't come from

work." Olya looked questioningly at the experimenter, who did not say anything.

Olya: "Kolya, go. Go to work."

Kolya went away, but in a few minutes he again approached the girls, anxious to join in the game. Ira took charge.

Ira: "We told you, you are still at work. Go back to work."

Kolya: "I am going on a business trip to Leningrad and I will write you a letter." He went to a table and started to "write" a letter. At this point, another child, Natasha, also with a doll-daughter, approached the girls.

Natasha: "Hello, I came to visit you. Let's get your children and go to the zoo."

Ira: "No, we won't go. My daughter is afraid of animals."

Natasha: "Oh! You don't say. Such a big girl and afraid of animals." (She smiled.)

Ira: "Yes, afraid."

Natasha: "It's shameful to be afraid. They are in cages. It wouldn't scare anyone."

Ira (after a pause): "My daughter is sick."

Natasha: "That's not so. You have a healthy one there. Let's go to the zoo."

Ira: "I said no. Go away, or your daughter will catch something from ours."

Natasha: "Yes, she's already sick with this illness."

Ira (pushing Natasha aside with a shove): "Go away, or your daughter will infect ours. Go away, fast." (Natasha was forced to leave.)

The experimenter analyzed the situation as containing three conflicts. The first conflict was the inclusion or exclusion of other children in the game. Looba, for example, did not know how to play with other children. He needed to be told what a doctor does, with specific actions like taking a temperature or listening to the heartbeat. He did not know how to coordinate his own role with that of the other children or how to react to active opposition to his participation in the game.

The second conflict was in the collision of subjects, and the way in which the children tried to get out of difficult positions.

Natasha introduced a new subject—going to the zoo. This initiated the complicated chain of events, the "defense of the subject." Ira and Olya had to defend their subject against Natasha's subject.

The third conflict came when the leader, Ira, in imitating the role of Mama and maintaining her leadership, did, in fact, imitate a real person whose authority was not to be questioned:

"I am the mama. I know best."

When Ira's role as leader was threatened she did not hesitate to change the basic situation. Although her doll had been the one who was supposedly sick, she suddenly changed her story in order to keep Natasha out of the game: "Go away, or your child will infect ours." Ira also resorted to physical force, by pushing Natasha aside.

Such primitive means of extricating themselves from conflicts as pushing, arguments, fights and other undesirable behavior are typical of children who have not learned how to play. Analyzing such behavior is easier than curing it, but analysis is at least the first step.

To escape from situations of conflicts, children resort to direct physical activity, complain to a grown person or start to cry, pass on to threats to leave the game, appeal to their position as leader of the game, change the subject of the game in such a fashion that it fits their assertions, or appeal to the objective reality of the limits of the game by saying, "That doesn't happen."

Since these patterns are only more primitive versions of the ones which occur in dealings among nations, it is not surprising that Soviet scientists have not yet found the complete answer to the problem, though they are working on it. It is similar to the question which was posed to the famous children's writer S. Y. Marshak by a group of five- and six-year-olds who were playing a very strenuous game. Marshak asked the children what they were playing, and they replied that they were fierce warriors, playing war.

"Playing war!" Marshak said, with displeasure. "You must know that our country is opposed to war. You had better play peace."

"*Ladno* [O.K.]," the children replied, stopping the game and looking at each other blankly. After a minute of silence, their leader stepped up to Marshak and asked politely:

"Dedushka [Grandfather], how do you play Peace?"

We had never seen a Soviet child with a toy gun until our last trip in 1969. There were still no toy guns in any of the kindergartens, but on the street we saw preschool children with long-barreled, wooden-handled guns. There were not many—perhaps one in a hundred children carried them—but we were surprised to see them, since on our previous trips, we had gathered that the Soviets were opposed to war toys. The new 1969 *Program of Education for the Kindergarten* also contained new material about the Soviet Army and the defense of the motherland. The children are taught to recognize infantrymen, sailors, flyers and artillerymen, and some dolls are dressed in military costumes.

In a small village outside Moscow we saw a group of Young Pioneers playing war games under apparently military guidance, and this too was the first time we had seen anything of this sort among the young people. We still saw no indication of war games in the kindergarten, but little children tend to imitate older ones. If Young Pioneers play war games, Little Octobrists will want to, also.

The Soviets have found that little children are definitely interested in what the older children are doing, but mixing the age groups demands careful planning. An older child instructed to play with a younger child needs specific suggestions on how to play. Playing, to the older child, may mean taking a spade away from a younger child who is playing in a sandbox, and asking the next day, "What do we take away from them today?"

The teacher must explain to the older child that the object of the game is to teach the younger child to do something for himself. The older child likes to teach the younger child independence, though he sometimes waits impatiently as the younger child goes through the motions of a new game slowly and laboriously. Often the younger child has no idea of how to play with an older child. A three-year-old who has not attended *yasli* often will prefer grownups to children. Others want to play with the older children but do not know how. Larisa loved to play with the older children, but she always broke every toy she picked up.

Lena, aged four years and two months, and Ira, two years and three months, had conflicting ideas of the goal of their activity. The two were busily engaged in putting building materials into a box. Lena explained: "We put cubes in here first, then bricks."

This fine distinction was completely lost on Ira, who began putting bricks into the box. Lena took them out and explained the rule again patiently. Ira again put bricks into the box. She could not understand Lena's demands or why the bricks were taken out of the box. Ira made one more energetic attempt to put the bricks in the box, an attempt again thwarted by Lena. This time Ira stopped work completely and busied herself with other things. Lena ran to the teacher and complained in exasperation, "Ira won't put away the cubes."

The older child must be a good example for the younger child to follow, and Soviet educators have also found that both children derive more benefit from the association if the older children visit the younger on a regular basis, though this is often difficult, due to conflicting schedules, quarantines for infectious diseases, and other disruptions.

Older children particularly liked playing the role of "Mama" to the younger children, but often were despotic in insisting that the younger ones fulfill their role as obedient children.

Creative role playing is at first very primitive. The child begins to rock her doll as she has seen her mother do with a younger child; then, imitating other actions of people around her, she "feeds" an animal or "drives" an automobile. In all the role playing the child is striving to be independent. *"Ya sam* [I (can do it) myself]," the normal child of two or three says when someone tries to help him. The Soviet psychologist Daniel Elkonin noticed that children whose attempts at independence had been thwarted by their parents or teachers did not know how to play or played very poorly.

Creative play with various materials, Elkonin calls "subject play," and he divided subject play into two parts: ready-made objects like toy animals, dolls, toy furniture, dishes, airplanes, automobiles, excavators and other easily identified objects, and building materials, including what grownups often call *musor* ("trash"). Sometimes Soviet children, like American children, value their trash more highly than their expensive toys, and Elkonin cautions Soviet parents to be considerate about inquiring before they throw away something that may be a cherished "subject" in role playing.

Children can also be very literal. Another Soviet educator gave some children blocks and pebbles to play with, and when she asked them what they were doing, they replied quite simply that they were playing with blocks and pebbles. Yet, when a definite game was suggested, the blocks and pebbles quickly became food, frying pans and plates and the children themselves became cooks and mamas.

The Soviet attitude toward the treatment of toys is typical of the Soviet ideology. When a toy is broken, the child is asked seriously, "Look, Milan, how you have spoiled this toy. Do you know how much work it took in the factory to make such a pretty autobus? And you have broken it so quickly! All of the children loved this autobus, and now they will not have a bus."

The social consequences of the broken toy are much more evident in the Soviet attitude than in the American attitude. The American teacher is more apt to say, "Now *you* won't get another toy, since you don't know how to take care of it." The American child has not betrayed his country by breaking the toy, and I think this attitude is one of the basic differences between the Soviet child and the American child. The American child is a future citizen of his country, while the Soviet child is considered a present citizen, with most of the responsibilities that citizenship entails. This makes his goals more like adult goals, while in the United States children's goals and adult goals are apt to be diametrically opposed.

The new 1969 *Program* hopes to increase this feeling of responsibility. Elkonin thinks that children express in their play the "cares of the country." The new *Program* will try to acquaint the child more fully with his country by making his impressions of life more concrete and extensive.

Knowledge is even more important in play with building materials. Unlike most play, construction has a goal. It develops the child's imagination and prepares him for work activities. It develops the thought processes of analysis and synthesis, which are still very weak in preschool children.

The building corner of every kindergarten is well supplied with material, so that each child has all he needs and wants. There are all sorts and sizes and colors of large and small building blocks, bricks, cubes, half cubes, prisms, cylinders and arches. Almost every kindergarten we saw had a larger-than-child-size Kremlin, magnificently built. The building corner always had toys children might need as adjuncts to their buildings—plastic or polyethylene animals, birds, toy people, machines and trucks. There was usually a large album of photographs showing the best models the children had made in their own kindergarten and another album of pictures of some of the best construction models of children from other parts of the Soviet Union.

Construction play has some of the elements of all the other types of play. It is creative (though the Soviet conception of true subject play involves relationships *between* people rather than the imitation of one activity of people as builders). It is also an active form of play, involving quite a lot of physical activity, using both large and small muscles. It develops the mind and requires initiative and a practical knowledge of how to use the hands. It is also compatible with the Communist emphasis on material production according to definite plans.

The very young child when first confronted with building material may treat it like a toy. One little tot, seeing her first brick, looked at it a long time then got out her handkerchief, wrapped it around the brick like a shawl and started to play with it as though it were a doll. The first manipulation of building materials by a very young child usually consists of picking the materials up, putting them in a wagon, and taking them somewhere else. Nechaeva calls this the "processional" activity of construction play.

For three-year-olds, Soviet teachers like the simpler forms of building materials. The first building project may consist of laying a railroad track, where bricks are laid more or less in a row. While they are learning to make a straight line the name of the game is often changed: today's railway track can become a streetcar line or a highway tomorrow, so the children feel they are trying something new, even while developing an old skill.

When they know how to build a straight line they make tables and chairs for dolls. Before showing them how to make a table and chairs, the teacher tells the children that the dolls are tired and want to sit down. She asks the children how the dolls can sit down and when the children suggest a chair, the teacher shows how to make one.

Soviet teachers are cautioned not to go too fast in suggesting complicated building projects. It was found that young children who were given building materials only, played contentedly about twice as long as children who were given building materials plus subject materials (materials to build a bridge and also an automobile to drive over the bridge). The presence of two materials diverted the second group's attention from the main task.

Another experiment showed that three-year-olds were usually too young to do something that required coordination of both hands, even in a favorite occupation like making mud pies. Out of twenty three-year-olds in one experiment, only seven made correctly formed mud pies. Four did not know how to tap the mold to get the pies out. Three forgot that before the pies could be removed from the mold, they had to pat the mud in tightly. Two, in turning the mold over, crushed the pies with their fingers. The unsuccessful workers threw mud at each other.

The child who does not receive satisfaction from his work or fails in the task loses interest, and his failure severely limits his future development. The Soviets are very interested to see that the child does not fail, and they feel that the teacher's task is to stimulate the child to want to succeed, then give him the knowledge necessary to success.

Not all children are interested in construction play. Some

prefer subject play. For these children, the teacher may suggest a building goal that involves subject play, such as building a house for the dolls. The children who lack independence and initiative must be encouraged by the teacher.

Some children just stand around and watch other children build things. A teacher took one such child and showed him an album of various constructions. The child looked through the book for some time, finally deciding that he wanted to build an airplane. When he had finished, the teacher showed his plane to the class and praised his work so that he would feel like building something else.

The older children can connect subject play and construction play very well, and when they have built a model of a subway or a public building, they play with it.

The Soviet Union has, in addition to its preschool institutions for normal children, special schools for blind, for deaf-mute and for mentally retarded children of preschool age. Yevpatoria, on the Black Sea, was built in 1936 by decree of the Council of People's Commissars (now called the Council of Ministers) especially for sick children. There are children's sanatoria, guesthouses for mothers with sick infants, sanatoria for teenagers, and pioneer camps.

In February 1960 the Russian minister of education opened a one-year preschool institution for blind children to prepare them for first grade. The Institute of Defectology of the Academy of Pedagogical Sciences of the U.S.S.R. began to study the problem too, in order to make recommendations for the training of blind children for school.

It was found that blind children, being much less active than sighted children, were less well developed physically, particularly in the small muscles of the arms and legs. The children themselves were afraid to move about freely, and their parents had strengthened the children's fears with their own fears that the children would hurt themselves if they moved about too freely.

In the kindergarten special gymnastics are given to the blind children. In teaching an exercise the teacher explains the exercise to the children then, standing behind a child, goes through the motions of the exercise with him, lifting the child's arms according to the instructions and in general showing him expressly how to do the exercise. When she has gone through this procedure with each child individually, the children are ready to do exercises as a group.

Since self-confidence is one of the goals as well as physical improvement, the teacher is careful to praise the children for their successes and to minimize their failures.

When the child first moves about the room the teacher clears a path for him, or tells him about obstacles. The furniture is specially made with round corners to minimize hurts. The wardrobe of each blind child is marked by a raised emblem which the child can feel with his hands—a fruit, vegetable or geometric figure that the child can recognize. It is very important that the child believe in his own ability to do things, so the furniture is in its accustomed place and the children are encouraged not only to walk but to run around as normal children do.

Jumping is difficult for blind children, so the first jumps are done in place, then they jump over a small barrier, holding on to the teacher's hand, then finally make jumps by themselves. They play games like "Hide from the Wolf" and "Don't Get your Feet Wet" (practice in lifting their feet, since blind children, if left to their own devices, are inclined to have a shuffling gait).

In other games—"Mice Run Tikho-Tikho [Quietly]" and "The Bear Takes Wide Steps"—they learn, by trying to imitate, the different kinds of movement, with the teacher helping when necessary. The new movements and exercises are built on the foundation of one already mastered, and soon the child can run about, climb stairs and do exercises.

Since the blind child's hearing is usually very keen, he learns to "watch" what he does with his ears. When he throws a ball he listens for the sounds it makes on landing, and the teacher tells him how close to the target he came. He throws pebbles into the water and listens to the splashes they make.

He also plays games that normal children enjoy—"Know Him by His Voice" and "Fisherman and Fish." He is encouraged to differentiate voices by sounds. Since physical contact is his main orientation with the world, he often learns to know a teacher first by the feel of her skirt.

Olya had grown accustomed to the feel of her teacher's corduroy skirt which Olya thought was very pretty. When the teacher changed to another dress Olya did not know her at first. Feeling the unfamiliar skirt she said hesitantly, "Is it you, Lidya Ivanovna? I didn't recognize you." The teacher reassured the child, and in a few days Olya said confidently, "Now I know you by your voice."

The sensory experience of the blind child is important. He learns to recognize vegetables, flowers and other familiar objects by their feel.

He is given a cat to hold, and the teacher says, "Stroke the cat's head. Now feel the cat's back and tail. What a long thin flexible tail he has. Can you feel how the cat arches its back under your fingers?"

As the child feels the paws, claws and other parts of the cat, he also learns new words.

Like normal children, the blind child learns the names of trees and flowers from their leaves and branches, and he must describe how one leaf differs from another. His powers of observation are strengthened by feel, smell and sound. He learns music, and through music appreciates a number of natural sounds—the sounds of rain, the babble of a brook; the beauty of everyday life.

Through all these experiences the blind child is learning his native language by ear, and now his hands become acquainted with the written word in Braille, beginning with the letters of the Braille alphabet.

The teacher tells the children about *one* and *many*, the beginning exercise in counting. In the next lesson they learn *two*, which comes after *one*, and so on up to *ten*. A typical lesson begins with the shape of the number, then the teacher gives the children a definite number of acorns or mushrooms, or something else they can feel, and asks them how many they have. Simple arithmetic begins when the teachers says, "Children, sit down on your chairs now. Sit deep in your seat with your backs straight." Correct posture is particularly emphasized with blind children. "I'm going to give you two baskets. We have to put seven mushrooms in two baskets. Tell me how we divide them."

When one child says, "Two in one basket and five in the other," the teacher asks another child to actually put the mushrooms in the baskets as the first child suggested. All possible combinations are divided, mentally and physically, and the children are praised for their correct results.

Counting, for blind children, is easier than some more abstract things which they cannot see. "Tall" and "wide" are taught by comparisons with things the children can feel for themselves, like the wardrobe where they hang their clothes or the width of the bench they sit on. A tall building, or a tall tree, is harder for them to visualize, so first they learn that a wardrobe is taller than a table, and a bench is wider than a pencil, and so more abstract relationships become clear to them.

Everything is done to avoid a feeling of inadequacy in the blind child. He must learn to do the things normal children do, but the task must not be too difficult in the beginning. In his work education, he may at first fill a bucket of water and pour it on some plants as the teacher says how thirsty the plants were and how much they appreciated a nice drink of water.

Before they undertake any task, the teacher says, "Let's think what we need to do to get ready for this job." "What will we do?" "How do we begin?" The children are taught to analyze the situation and then to follow the task through to the end.

Blind children are inclined to give up before fulfilling the task, so Soviet teachers encourage them to formulate a goal and fulfill it. The encouragement of the child's friends is particularly important when they engage in collective work.

In self-service—dressing and undressing—where definite rules are followed conducive to formation of orderly habits, the children are taught to button their clothes from the top down and to unbutton things from the bottom. The left shoe is put on first. The clothes are laid out in a definite place each time and placed in the same order each time.

Order is also one of the principles of aesthetic education for blind children. It is a step toward the realization of the word *beautiful,* which the children must feel in their relations with nature, art and music. The beauty of music is easy for them to understand, as is the beauty of the native fairy tales and stories that they are told and encouraged to tell themselves.

The blind children are permitted to feel elaborate filigree work by an old master or asked to feel the beauty of the stitches in some embroidery. In conversations with the teacher on their walks about their town they are told of the beautiful buildings, the shops, the factories. Wherever possible they feel for themselves, but they also see things through the eyes of the teacher.

They learn to model with clay and to paste applications on paper, developing the fine muscles of their fingers and hands. They make baskets and construct other useful objects.

Like normal children, the blind children learn to orient to their surrounding world, to other people and to themselves. They are encouraged to help each other, to contribute to the collective. The Soviets try to take a medium course between two harmful extremes—the one where parents and teachers rob the blind child of all initiative by doing too much for him and the other extreme where the child is pushed beyond his capabilities.

The Soviets believe that the blind child can do almost anything a sighted child can, although his education must be specialized and geared to his deficiency. Like the normal child, he too must become a member of the collective.

·VI·

The Collective

THE FAMILY IS the Soviet child's first collective. Soviet educators admit that usually the child grows properly under family conditions, even though no particular system of education is followed. He learns to walk and talk. He imitates his older brothers and sisters and the grownups in his family. He is happy and healthy. Why, then, should he go to a *yasli* or *detsky sad*?

The obvious fact that most mothers work is not necessarily a compelling reason for sending the child to a preschool institution. There is a tremendous supply of grandmothers in the Soviet Union, and most young couples either live with their parents or send their children to live with them or have one of the child's grandmothers living with them. The typical "family" consists of mother, father, grandmother and child (or children).

The grandmother—or *babushka,* as she is called in Russian—is an important institution in her own right. Since Soviet women retire at fifty-five with a pension of from fifty-five to one hundred percent of their wages, the grandmother is still young enough to cope with grandchildren, and her pension helps the family income. If she has had five or more children and a work record of fifteen years, the grandmother may retire at fifty.

"My mother would be bored if she did not have my children to take care of," one guide told us, explaining one of the reasons her child did not go to nursery school. The grandmother thinks that she is completely competent to teach the young child, often feeling that she can do a better job than *yasli* or *detsky sad.* "Why, there are children in the oldest group of kindergarten who don't know where their left hand is and where their right hand is. It is ridiculous," one said contemptuously of her rival the kindergarten.

We saw these sweet but firm grandmothers everywhere. In spring they and their grandchildren come out in the parks before the crocuses, walking hand in hand leisurely, or stopping to buy ice cream or to buy something to put in the string bag every Russian carries, since the stores have no paper bags for their products.

One favorite place for grandmother-and-child viewing in Moscow is Durov's Corner, a small theater specializing in animal acts, which caters particularly to grandmothers and grandchildren. On Saturdays the menagerie around the theater and the lobby are jammed with grandmothers and children. Their excited voices are high and tense—"Wait!" "Hurry up!" "Mustn't do that." "Over here!" When an attendant finally says *"Syuda, Tovarishi.* [This way, Comrades]," they surge through the opened doors, the children to the front rows of seats and the grandmothers in the back. Some of the children glance back apprehensively at the grandparents, who lean forward encouragingly—"Don't be afraid. I'm right here."

The house lights go out, and the excitement subsides with a sibilant *"Vsyo, vsyo"* from the grandparents, which means that

everything is all right. The grandmothers settle down like hens on a nest, only to pop up now and then with some admonition to a child. The acts on the stage are charming. A raccoon raises a flag, a fox rings a bell and plays a xylophone, a monkey reads a book and counts on an abacus. A cat walks a tightrope, and a rooster and a fox eat out of the same dish. A German shepherd dog does arithmetic. Everyone has a marvelous time, the children watching the animals, the grandparents watching the grandchildren, my husband and I watching all three.

On Sunday the grandmothers really come into their glory and irritate the Soviet state the most. Many of them go to church and take their little grandchildren with them, despite the signs blazoned in public buildings, RELIGION IS THE OPIATE OF THE PEOPLE. It is against the law to give religious instruction to children under eighteen, although the Soviet Constitution guarantees freedom of religious worship. The Constitution also guarantees freedom of antireligious propaganda. Most towns have museums of atheism and *znanie* ("knowledge") societies to combat religion, and the magazine *Nauka i Religiya* (*Science and Religion*) is constantly explaining how unscientific religion is.

Special meetings are held throughout the Soviet Union to educate grandmothers in atheism. Seventy-eight grandmothers attended one such meeting. They heard reports on antireligious ideas and saw children give experiments "exposing" religion. At the end of the program, each grandmother was given a picture of Lenin and a leaflet on atheism. *Nauki i Religiya* reported that the "touched grandmothers thanked the children and the teachers in short speeches. They promised not to prevent the schools from educating the children in their families as atheists."

Occasionally the antireligious meetings backfire. One lecturer, cautioned not to be boring, was describing the creation of the cosmos in glowing but scientific terms. He was delighted with the rapt attention of his audience until one old woman said to him, admiringly, "See how cleverly everything in the world is arranged! And they say there is no God!"

At the Victory of October Factory, in Ryazan, there were not enough places in the kindergarten for all the children, and the grandmothers in the town were asked to baby-sit so the mothers could work. The grandmothers got together and issued an ultimatum: "We won't baby-sit for unchristened children. If you let them be christened we'll come and baby-sit." The account of the revolt ended reassuringly: the atheists of Ryazan came to the rescue, and the "old women's plot" was thwarted.

Despite articles in *Pravda* and *Izvestia* asking for a harder line against religious superstitions, the churches are usually full of people, and we saw many more babies being christened on our last trip than we saw on our first. We even heard one or two girls say, "Wedding palaces are common. I want to be married in a church." Most of the congregations are old, however, and young people are inclined to think religion is a boring occupation of the old.

Such metaphysical considerations have no place in the official moral doctrines of the Soviet state. Soviet morality is based on the collective, where each member works for the good of all. The good, happy family is, on a larger scale, the ideal of the collective, and a happy family is an important Soviet ideal. Many Westerners think that collectivism means the stifling of individuality, but the Soviets deny this. They say that the true collective brings out the best in the individual and that it is important for him to develop as an individual so that he may contribute more to the collective. The difference is in the goal. The Soviets feel that the "bourgeois" world develops the individual for selfish ends, while the Soviet individual is developed for the good of society in general.

This idea is particularly expressed in the difference in approach to the child's responsibilities. An American child is apt to have a choice which does not involve his feeling of responsibility to society. A popular American approach is to say to the child, "It is raining. You cannot go outside without your galoshes. If you do not want to wear your galoshes, stay inside. You may choose, but you may not go out without your galoshes."

In the Soviet Union the feeling is that many things must be done because they are right, and a choice is not always open to the child. In the above example the Soviet would say, "You need some outdoor exercise, but since it is raining, you must wear your galoshes, because you will catch a cold if you don't."

The objection to Montessori is similar. The Soviets say that in the Montessori system, since the child may choose his own activity (within the limit of the system), he is most apt to choose something that he does well already, while, according to the Soviet view, he needs to do something he doesn't already know how to do, and this probably will be something he also dislikes.

Discipline, Makarenko and his *bezprizornyi* found, enabled the whole collective to attain its aim, and through discipline each member had more security in his rights and responsibilities. The children in Makarenko's colonies had had bitter experience with undisciplined lives before they came to the colonies, so they were particularly grateful for the order which discipline brought.

"Discipline," Makarenko said, "is a product of the sum total of the creative efforts, including the teaching process, the process of political education, the process of character shaping, the process of collision—that is, facing and settling conflicts in the collective—the process of friendship and trust, and the whole educational process in its entirety, counting also such processes as physical education, phyical development, and so on."

Makarenko believed that the interests of the collective are superior to those of the individual, and that discipline must be an adornment of the collective. The tradition was always to give the hardest task to the best detachment. Makarenko believed that discipline would help a person take pleasure in doing a necessary, unpleasant task, and he felt that Soviet society differed from other societies in that the Soviet state placed higher demands on its citizens than did bourgeois society. Place the utmost demands upon a person, and treat him with the utmost respect.

The Soviets are very much interested in how the collective helps the formation of desired social feelings and how it interferes with them. In one experiment dealing with this question, the children of an experimental group were divided into three categories. The children who fulfilled their tasks well without having to be reminded by the teacher were put into group one. The children in group two tried to fulfill their tasks conscientiously, but needed some external support, either from the teacher or from their comrades. The children in group three, while having a sense of responsibility, needed positive external support and were deeply distressed by any negative evaluation of their work. The children in group one worked quickly and efficiently within their own group, but when mingled with the children from group three the association proved harmful to both groups. The group-three children, observing the obvious abilities of the first group, became agitated and nervous. They tried to hurry beyond their skills, and their work became worse and worse and frequently was abandoned altogether. The first group, in turn, was distracted by the slower children, and their work too suffered. The middle group of children were found to mix well with either the top or the bottom group. With the first group, the middle group accepted help and advice, improving their own performances from the experience of the better-skilled children. Similarly, when placed with the lower group, the middle children appeared to give confidence to the less skilled and to help them upgrade their work.

The teacher must see that the children who play and work together receive mutual benefit from the association. Younger children, although proud to play with older children, often need the teacher's help and advice on specific matters, such as how to catch the ball the older child has thrown.

On an excursion an older child can point out interesting aspects of nature to the younger child, or at school can teach him to build a house or can tell him a story or perform some other specific task. Satisfaction from cooperation strengthens the solidarity of the group collective.

Some of the five-to-seven-year-olds, in preparing to help the younger children, simply worried about them instead of playing with them. It was found that one of the important motives of both groups was simply the desire to "be good," but the educators found that this desire, by itself, was not enough. The abstract idea of being good must be emphasized in concrete situations.

Specific expressions of sympathy are taught. If a small child has fallen down, an older child is sent to comfort him in a particular way. The dirt is shaken from the child's clothes, and the older child says, "Don't cry. Let's play. Here is a toy for you"; or the older child is advised to show the younger child a fish in the aquarium or some other diversion.

Sharing of toys is important in the collective, but if the older child feels he really needs a particular toy that a younger one wants, he may offer the younger child another toy, saying politely, "I'll play with this just a little longer. Here's a doll for you." If this does not work and there is a crisis, the younger child is usually allowed to prevail, since the older child, being more mature, also has more responsibility.

The three-year-old who has come directly from home and has not been to *yasli*, is often more drawn to grownups than to other children, and such a child is often not prepared for the kindergarten's collective society. He does not know how to play with others and to share.

These children often have a favorite toy to which they cling tightly with no thought of sharing with other children. They do not initiate play with others and are far behind the children who have been "collectivized" at an earlier age, by sharing playpens, toys and experiences. Their play is still so simple that there isn't even a place for another child.

One such child, Vanya, a three-year-old boy, new to the kindergarten, was busy making a boat for himself with no apparent thought for or interest in those around him. The teacher wanted to bring the child into the collective, so she asked him to show her the boat when he had finished it. When he brought it to her she said, "What a beautiful boat. A nice boat like this should sail somewhere, but before it can sail it needs a captain and a crew."

"I'll be the captain," Vanya said.

"You need a crew, though," the teacher said. "Now where

The sea has a great fascination for Soviet children. These sailors at Tashkent's Kombinat 208 are clearly identified in the word "sailor" embroidered in gold on their caps. The red-and-white life preserver carries the Russian word for peace.

can we find some children for the crew?" She looked around her at the other kindergarten children, and Vanya looked too, apparently seeing the other children for the first time. One or two children had come up to listen to the conversation, and one boy volunteered as a crew member.

"I don't know," the teacher said doubtfully; but Vanya said positively, "Yes, yes."

The game progressed finally to a more concrete situation. The boat set out for Rumania, complete with captain, crew and passengers. After an exciting storm at sea, the passengers disembarked in Rumania, where they bought presents for their relatives and friends. On their return home the travelers were met at the dock by their friends, a festive band and much flag waving. One by one, the teacher had drawn all of the children into the game, and Vanya had become part of the collective society.

Playing together involves complicated mental processes which must be carefully nurtured by teachers and parents. An educational article tells how one teacher drew another child, Oleg, into the collective. Oleg preferred to play alone, refusing to accept the teacher's suggestions that he play with the other children. He had his own project of building a dam and a large canal, and he attacked the project with energy, working at it over a period of several days. One day the teacher noticed that Oleg was looking at his dam with evident dissatisfaction.

"How is your work going?" she asked.

"*Ne ochen* [Not very well]," Oleg said despondently.

"Really?" the teacher said. "In my opinion, it's an easy matter. If you joined your canal to Ivan's you could have a huge one."

A flicker of interest showed in Oleg's eyes, and the teacher turned to the others: "Children, how can we join our canal with Oleg's? Perhaps we can choose workers and they will dig canals to meet."

All the children united in the common goal, and the work went faster. "I" and "mine" became "we" and "ours." The common work created an atmosphere of emotional enthusiasm and created good feelings.

Krupskaya said that the earlier a child lived a collective life, the greater the chance that he would grow up to be a real Communist, and today's Soviet educators think that only in the collective can you create the characteristics necessary for the multisided development of the desired new man.

If the child's family influences have been good, the child comes to *yasli* or *detsky sad* with a basic feeling for the collective. In one group of fifty-nine children, twenty percent were friendly with teachers as well as other children, seldom quarreled, and wanted to do what was best for the group. Sixty-nine percent of the children were good in school, but at home often disregarded parents' instructions or quarreled with brothers or sisters. Eleven percent quarreled frequently, complained often, and were more interested in themselves than in the group. For the bad conduct of the latter group the parents were blamed.

Many Soviet parents have the feeling that "I worked hard; let my child be happy." Soviet educators deplore this feeling. "Happiness is not just working for yourself," they keep repeating. "Happiness is working for others." Morality is learned in everyday activities, in games as well as in work, and since the Soviets define morality as a form of social consciousness, morality is developed in the collective, on the foundation of feelings of sympathy.

The first moral feeling begins with the feeling the child has for its mother. It is a quick feeling of identification with another person. The child shows it as early as his first conscious smile, and later when he hands his toy to someone he is showing the first desire to share. The feeling of conscious sympathy does not come until later, and the child of even three or four when asked why he must not fight will answer, "Because you'll get hit in the eye," or, "The police will arrest you."

The *yasli* and *detsky sad* teachers believe that in the orderly, organized school the child soon learns what is good and what is bad. First he learns a few basic rules: don't throw toys; ask politely for a toy; don't grab it; put your toy back in place after playing with it. One teacher, E. K. Strekalova, concluded that to have an organized, friendly collective, certain rules must be established and a clear-cut regime must be followed.

Makarenko said the child's will was not simply a wish and its satisfaction, but a wish and its renunciation at the same time; without a brake, the child's will could not develop properly. In practice, we were told, the child develops his own brake in a process of work and play that is interesting to him. The rules are for his benefit too.

The children perform "emotional gymnastics" as they play "You Are a Brave Cosmonaut" or "You Are a Merry Clown" or "You Are a Kind Nurse," until, by assuming the role, the child learns the accompanying emotions. When the child is afraid he puts on his "brave face," and when he is hurt he makes a "merry face." Perhaps we do not cry when we are sad, but are sad because we cry.

Starting in early childhood every effort is made to teach the children to control senseless rages, fear, and other harmful emotions. The emotional training of the child should be started by the time he is two or three. The first step is to make the child feel secure as a member of the collective. To do this, the older members must understand his needs. His early cries and shouts are cries for help, before he can use words, to indicate that he is hungry or wet or uncomfortable.

The older child too may seem obstreperous when he really has some need which is not being met. Serozha, just over a year old, fell to his knees and lay down on the floor every day when the other children were beginning to have dinner. Since he lay on the floor only before dinner, the teacher thought he must be expressing some kind of protest. She found that he, as one of the older babies, had to wait for the second "sitting" at dinner. When he was invited to eat with the younger babies he cheerfully went to the table, where he ate peacefully with good appetite. His lie-in had accomplished its purpose.

Another child, Kolya, cried every time the nursery school started for a walk. After a talk with Kolya's mother, the teacher discovered that Kolya's obstreperousness had started in October when his mother bought him some new shoes. Further investigation revealed that the shoes were too tight and uncomfortable. The child, foreseeing an unpleasant sensation when he put on his shoes, simply refused to get dressed for a walk. With comfortable shoes he was as merry as anyone on the walk.

The little child who has few words with which to express himself (and those not readily understood by others) shows his unhappiness in crying, shouting or withdrawal. Occasionally children become obstreperous when they are unable to fulfill the task the teacher has set for them, or when they have been asked to sit still too long. Everything should be checked before blaming the child for his bad behavior.

The Russians are very tolerant of what they call *kapriz* (caprice). Caprice is defined as "a senseless whim," or "conduct deprived of a rational foundation," but it is typical of the behavior of small children everywhere. The Russians have many books on the obstreperous child, and even a little musical play which delights parents and children. In the play a little girl, howling loudly, swallows Caprice, a *bukazlyuka* (bogeyman), who makes her very uncomfortable until she decides to be a good girl again and says, "I don't want to be capricious."

Sometimes the basis of undesirable behavior in the child is due to the discrepancy between the child's demands and his ability to live up to those demands. The sheer impossibility of achieving may lead the child to constant failure, and his inadequate reactions further arouse his dissatisfaction when he sees other children making satisfactory adjustments. The child cannot accept the fact that his inadequate reactions are due to his own weakness, so he strikes out at those around him.

The child needs to maintain his self-esteem, either through personal satisfaction in his abilities or through the approval of parents or teachers. Occasionally the child will have too high a self evaluation. Marina, who lived with a doting but psychotic mother, when asked if she liked the other children in her class said she didn't, because they were bad. "And you?" the experimenter said.

Marina: "I'm good. It seems to me that they are bad, and I am good. It seems to me that I am better than they are. Everyone thinks she is better than everyone else."

Experimenter: "No, not everyone. Many children say that they are not the best."

Marina: "But I think that I am."

Experimenter: "That you are what?"

Marina: "I'm better than everyone."

Experimenter: "What does that mean, 'better than everyone'?"

Marina: "Better, best of all."

Experimenter: "And kinder?"

Marina: "And kindest of all."

Experimenter: "Really, isn't Tanya the kindest in the class?"

Marina: "She is kind, but I am kinder."

Experimenter: "And who is better. You or Tanya?"

Marina: "I think that I am."

Experimenter: "And do the other girls acknowledge that you are smarter, kinder and better?"

Marina: "No."

Experimenter: "Do they see that you are?"

Marina: "They see, of course."

Experimenter: "Why don't they acknowledge it?"

Marina was thin, small and sickly. She was very quiet and did not joke with the other children. She tried hard to do well, but her continual arguments with the other children ended in tears. During free-play periods, Marina stood off by herself, watching the other children, or looking at a book. She was always complaining to the teacher about the other children, or trying to tell the children what they should do, though they ignored her completely. Even though she tried hard, her grades were threes and sometimes two. (Five is the top grade.) Marina was not part of the collective. Her mother, with her constant praise, had given her a false evaluation of herself.

When Marina entered the first grade her problem became worse, until the teachers began a correction program designed to give her a more realistic self-appraisal and still an evaluation with which she could live. Marina was drawn into the collective through a friend, and as part of the collective she could share the pride of the collective's achievement and gradually make some contribution of her own.

The child learns the rules in kindergarten and is expected to know them, but the Soviets also stress the "education of the heart." Does a little boy give up his seat on the streetcar to an old woman because he has learned the rules or because he sees that the old woman is tired? The Soviets hope the child follows the rules out of the goodness of his heart.

Children must learn to obey, but the adult's demands must

be reasonable. The folk tale of the old man who told the boy to plant cabbages, roots up, is a story Soviets use to illustrate false training. The boy, obediently planted the cabbages upside down as he was told to do, but after planting them, he could not resist asking the old man, "When I plant cabbages upside down, what will grow, old man?"

"Obedience, my son, obedience," said the old man.

The mutual respect and consideration which Communism extols is not always evident in the personal relations of the older generation. Clerks in stores, waitresses in restaurants, and others serving the public are constantly being criticized in the Soviet press for their rudeness, indifference, and lack of cooperation. Rudeness from a clerk prompts the Soviet citizen to ask, "What is Communist about you, Comrade?"

So that the upcoming generation will be better, kindergarten children practice Communist morality in everyday services, in their play. In Tashkent a group of children were playing "store," when Alesha, seeing a truck she liked, simply helped herself to it and walked out of the store without paying for it.

"That's not the way to do it," her playmates complained indignantly. "You grabbed the machine and didn't pay. You didn't even say, 'Thank you' or 'Goodbye.'"

The teacher said that stores were for buying things, that Alesha could not take what she wanted but must have money to pay for it. She suggested Alesha try again. This time, Alesha asked politely if she might buy the truck, and the other children smiled their approval. Alesha thanked the "saleslady" and left with her purchase, obviously quite pleased with herself.

One of the favorite lessons includes two age groups. The older children are told they will select a toy from the *chudesnyi meshochek* ("magic bag") to give to each younger child. When all the children have a toy, they play with it for three or four minutes, and then the teacher suggests that they all exchange toys, with an appropriate remark, like, *"Na* [Here you are], Valya, a rabbit."* Saying the name of the recipient and the name of the gift strengthens the action and gives it more importance as well as strengthening the identity of the child named. At first the children are inclined just to say *"Na"*; but soon even the

Playing with dolls is an important part of collective education.

recipient insists on the complete phrase.

Next, the older children suggest an activity: "Here is a doll named Masha, to greet you. Take her in your arms." Then the older child says, "Play with little Masha awhile and then give her to Karya." In the last exercise a few of the children must wait until it is their turn for the doll. They learn self-control and also watch to see how the other children observe the rules of the game. The waiting exercise often fails to work if the children are all three-year-olds. One child did not want to give up the doll to the child entitled to it next. Instead, he ran to the toy corner and picked up another toy, which he threw to Ira. Ira, knowing her rights, would not take the new toy, and the teacher had to intercede.

Most of the teachers we talked to commented that the three-year-olds were "very emotional" and that the norms of conduct have not yet become rules for them, though they are at an age when they value the adult *"Khorosho* [Good]" and are upset by the word *"Plokha* [Bad]."

Some Soviet parents say, "My child is very nervous. I can't do a thing with her," or, "This is some kind of tyrant, not a child." Such parents are advised by the Soviet writer Prosorov to deal with a kicking, crying child in a calm manner—"You know, crying is not allowed in this room. If you can't do without it, go into the bedroom, and there you can cry and be as capricious as you like."

Another Prosorov suggestion is to bring a looking glass to the crying child: "Look in the mirror and see what you have become." Prosorov does not promise that the mirror trick will work every time. Sometimes, he says philosophically, the crying child will look in the mirror and start to cry even harder.

The noted teacher, V. Verasaeva, recalled how her grandfather broke her of the habit of crying. One day he gave her a small glass bottle and said, "Collect your tears in this bottle, and when it is full I will pay you twenty kopeks for it."

Verasaeva agreed, thinking of the chocolate bars the money would buy, but she found that when she started to cry, she forgot about the bottle, and when she finally remembered the bottle—"What vexation! For some reason the tears had stopped their flow."

Russian children, as well as American children, know the "social value of tears." A child says, "I'm not crying to you, but to Auntie," or he doesn't cry at all when he falls down and hurts himself when no one is there to witness the tears. Another child will say, "With Grandmother, I don't cry." When asked "Why?", he raises his hands in the air and shrugs—"Useless."

The sympathetic response the Soviets want between parent and child, is illustrated by the story of Vasya. Vasya's mother was late coming home from work one night, and she found Vasya already in bed asleep. On the kitchen table were empty milk cartons—which surprised her, since Vasya was normally neat and usually put the empty cartons in the trash. When she leaned over to kiss Vasya good night, she noticed that he had toothpaste on his face. The next morning she asked him why he had not washed his face before going to bed.

"I did it on purpose," Vasya said, "so that you could see that I had brushed my teeth." Suddenly the mother realized that the empty milk cartons had also sent a message: "Don't worry, Mother. I drank my milk."

Vasya is the type of child the Soviets are trying to create—a responsible member of the collective. But how to create such a child is a problem Nechaeva and other members of the Preschool Institute are constantly investigating. They find the kindergartens are not succeeding one hundred percent in creating such children, despite their efforts.

Even though the children are taught to respect their toys and dolls from an early age, there is still evidence of toys being broken through neglect. Not all children are willing to sacrifice their own wishes to help a comrade; some children play together better than they work together, and some of the child leaders are not as friendly to their comrades as they should be. All of these problems concern the members of the Institute, who feel that it is not enough just to make out a list of desirable qualities. They must also create proper conditions for the development of these qualities.

Since example is one of the most important influences on children, parents and teachers are urged to set the children a good example, but the highest Communist morality is usually shown in the example of Lenin and his relations with his family. The year 1970 marks the one hundredth anniversary of Lenin's birth, so throughout the year emphasis on Lenin is heightened even more than usual.

The educators believe that before you can love something you must know it well, so the child is taught about Lenin through visits to the Lenin museum, through books and pictures. movies, slides and talks. It was Krupskaya herself who warned teachers against presenting Lenin as a "goody-good" child. In her article, "Teaching Lenin and Leninism in School" she wanted Lenin shown as he really was—not as an ikon to be worshiped, but rather like a pleasant grandfather who is interested in the children—"Lenin's grandchildren," as the kindergarten children are often called. Lenin is shown as a man concerned about the way his grandchildren will grow up and the way they fit into the collective.

·VII·

Socially Useful Labor

"How do we teach Marxism?" The director of a kindergarten in Sochi smiled at us. "Americans always want to know that." She laughed at the absurdity of a question I had not asked, but, being American, was expected to ask.

I had not asked the question, because I thought I knew the answer. Soviet kindergartens teach Marxism the way Krupskaya said she taught it to the working people before the Revolution —she taught Marxism without mentioning the name of Marx.

Marxism actually begins for the Soviet child with the first bright toy that is dangled over his crib. This toy represents socially useful labor, and later on the child will learn to respect the toy not just because it is pretty and fun to play with, but because of the respect due to the people who have made it. Communism is a system of social relationships, and inanimate objects are valued for the amount of personal labor that went into them and their relationships with people.

The child is also receiving an emotional conditioning toward labor, and this conditioning becomes an important component of his personality. Just as Makarenko found in building up his collective, work undertaken as a necessity for existence had a crucial impact on emotional growth.

Soviet educators believe that the child does not naturally love labor, but must be taught and encouraged to work. The Soviet people too were not conditioned to work, at the time of the Revolution. Years of serfdom and repression had conditioned them to devious ways of getting out of work, and many of these work characteristics still plague the leaders responsible for fulfillment of various plans. A survey found that what workers liked best about their jobs was the association with other workers. They preferred the "social" part to the "useful" part of socially useful labor. Many workers were discouraged when they learned that if they overfulfilled a plan one year, their norm for the next year was raised. One lady we met said she could not get eggs after September, because, her egg man said, "we have already fulfilled our plan for the year."

To combat attitudes like that the preschool child is carefully and methodically taught the value of work. Oddly enough, work was not always stressed in the early days of Soviet education. In the early days mechanical ideological indoctrination often confused the child. One child who had been told about Stalin building socialism saw some carpenters working on a roof and said, "Look how many Stalins there are on the roof."

In the thirties and forties there was a "work corner" in the kindergarten, where various materials and tools were kept, but there was no emphasis on the moral content of work or its influence on the child's personality. Although E. A. Arkin, A. P. Usova and others did some work on the problems of labor education of children, the emphasis in kindergarten was on the physical development and health of the child rather than on his labor record. In 1948 there was not a single article on work in the magazine *Doshkolnoye Vospitanie (Preschool Education)*.

Today, the child is not expected to do socially useful labor until he is two years old, but he is conditioned to labor even before that, starting with the bright toy hung over his crib. The toy attracts his attention.

Soviet pedagogues feel that building the attention span is the first step toward creating good working habits. The child's first attention for the toy hanging over his crib is involuntary. He is attracted by bright objects, loud noises or movement in front of him. When the toy is moved with some accompanying sound, the child is more attracted to it than when it is stationary. Initially, the interest the child shows in the toy is due to the organization on the part of the adult. The adult must make the project interesting to the child so that the child's attention becomes voluntary rather than involuntary.

Interest is built upon knowledge. The more the child knows about a subject the more interested he becomes and the easier it is for him to lengthen his attention span. By the first year of kindergarten his attention span should be sufficiently fortified so that the child can give his attention to something that in itself may be unattractive, but which is necessary for mastering some subject like reading or arithmetic. Soviet educators are more concerned with building up the ability to learn than they are in teaching kindergarten children to read and count.

At first the baby can't do very much except pay attention. He has to be fed and dressed, but he is also assimilating certain impressions of orderliness, friendliness and other sensations from his surroundings. He begins to assert his independence by wanting to do something for himself—he helps to hold his cup of milk or he reaches for the spoon that holds his cereal.

In the *yasli* these signs of independence are encouraged. Self-service is the first form of work. Instead of feeding the little child herself, the nurse will often put his bowl and spoon in front of him while she feeds a younger child. At first the child may cry as he watches the other child being fed first. Then he notices his food in front of him and dips a finger into his own bowl. The nurse puts the spoon in his fist and eventually some food gets on it. He licks the back of the spoon, dips it in the bowl again and eventually learns to eat by himself.

Dressing is the next form of work. When the two-year-old first begins to button his clothes it may take him fifteen minutes, and he may do it incorrectly, but he learns by practice. Dressing and undressing his dolls also helps him to learn to dress himself. If he is coming in from outdoors, or is going out for a walk, he dresses in a locker room, each age group having his own locker room. If he is dressing or undressing for his afternoon nap he undresses just inside the sleeping veranda, the clothes being neatly piled on little chairs in the room next to the sleeping veranda.

The little child has trouble distinguishing work from play. At first the process of buttoning is more interesting than the results, but gradually the child learns to achieve order, to button his

Little children may require some adult assistance at dinner, but they are encouraged to feed themselves. Soviet preschools give each child breakfast, dinner (served in the middle of the day), and a hearty snack (served in the mid-afternoon). Children who live at the school are also given supper.

buttons from the top down, to unbutton them from the bottom up, and to see that his shoes are "looking at each other."

Often a new four-year-old who has not been to *yasli* will not be as competent as a three-year-old with *yasli* experience. Sometimes the newcomer will say, "I don't want to do it. I don't know how to do it. I won't do it."

The teacher will say, "The other children are dressed and playing, and you sit here bored. I will teach you how to dress and then you can play too." No more than the most necessary help is given. The parents are asked to dress their children in clothes that are easy to put on and take off, and the children are shown how to manage for themselves.

The rules are not repeated over and over. A reminder such as "And how does Mashenka dress?" seems to work, and when the right answer is given, the teacher says, "Correct. You remembered well how Mashenka dresses."

After the child learns the rules, he is expected to conform to them. The children are expected to dress for a walk in eight to ten minutes. Those who dress more quickly are allowed to go out in the courtyard alone to wait for the others, though the teacher usually suggests a specific game for them to play while they wait.

The first real work experiences come next. The children imitate the work of the adults they know. The girls wash their dolls' clothes and clean their toys, while the boys repair toy trucks and feed plastic animals.

The process of forming correct attitudes toward work is carefully thought out. Preschoolers must learn to formulate a goal, find the correct path toward achieving the goal, and get results corresponding to the goal. The goal may at first be suggested by the teacher, but the "goal" of Soviet education is to stimulate the child to form his own goals and to persist in achieving them.

Three-year-old Vitya swung his shovel back and forth over a clean path as though he were shoveling snow. Although the activity was what the Soviets call a "processional activity," it had some useful features. The child, imitating adults, was learning how to hold a shovel, but the activity lacked a goal. One was furnished when the teacher suggested that he move to a path containing snow, where the same movements accomplished the removal of the snow from the path. The teacher praised his work and from then on Vitya lost interest in activities of only processional character, since attainment of a goal is much more interesting.

The goal must be within the ability of the child and must be near at hand. It should also be one that can be accomplished in a short time. Work in the garden has too distant a goal for the very young child. He cannot associate planting the seed with the harvest until he is at least six.

Two- and three-year-olds often set themselves unobtainable goals, and in those cases the teachers step in with assistance, though they are cautioned to help in such a way that the child is not made to feel even more helpless. The teacher may make the children think they are extricating her from a difficult position.

"Really, we helped you a little. It was hard for you to do it alone," the children should say.

With goal planning, children are encouraged to finish their work to the end and, if possible, collectively. Very young children do not engage in collective work with any regularity, so the teacher may have all the children perform independent actions until clean-up time, when each child puts his toys away with the others.

Even five-year-olds need to have their goals formulated by the teacher except in thoroughly familiar situations. They can formulate such goals as putting the bookshelf in order or cleaning up the building material, but more complicated goals need to be suggested by the teacher. Often the time spent explaining the goal and the process of attaining the goal takes more time than the actual work itself, but the Soviets are satisfied if these explanations lead to a correct attitude toward labor.

Another educational problem develops when the children know the goal but do not proceed correctly toward attainment of the goal. When the goal was watering the plants and one child was asked what he must do, he said, "I must bring water and pour it on the plants." But, when asked which he would do first, he said, "Pour it on the plants."

The way the goal is presented often has a bearing on the implementation of the goal. In one experiment kindergarten children were asked to make a rug for their mothers out of cut paper strips woven together. The teacher outlined the project. "You, Petya, make the purchases. You, Natasha, cut out the strips. Zhenya, you can glue the pieces together. We will make this rug together."

The children were shown a model of a finished rug, and the operations for making the rug were explained in succession. Then a picture of a little girl presenting a finished rug to a pleased mother was shown to the children. The children started the project enthusiastically, but were soon bored with cutting the strips, and began talking among themselves. In five minutes they abandoned the whole project.

An experimental group, given the same project, were told

how the mother praised her child for being able to cut out such straight strips and how lovely the rug looked when made of such strips. These children were advised that the mother would examine the rug, noticing straight or uneven strips. The experimenters noted that this group cut and painted strips for twenty-five to thirty minutes as against the first group's five minutes. The second group also made a much-better-looking rug.

With the first group, the motive (to make a present for mother) and the goal (to make good strips) were given at the same time, but independently of each other, while the second group was given a motive which was connected with the goal from the very beginning. Eventually the children are taught to make this connection for themselves.

Playing the roles of mothers and children, the "mothers" say they will not accept an ugly rug with uneven strips. The children discuss the methods of work and soon learn to analyze the necessary steps before beginning a project. The experimenters found that the child who could analyze and plan his work before beginning it worked more diligently and did better work.

Before starting any project the children discuss it. The teacher may say, "Now, what do we need to make a chair?" and the children say, "We need boards, hammer, and nails." To the question "How many boards?" the answer was: "Four—or no, five; one large one and four small."

When work is finished the results are studied and criticized. "Look how clean I washed the ball. It was *so* dirty." Or a child may say of another, "He didn't know how to do it," or "He didn't try."

The Soviet goal is that the child will love his work, and work is not used as a punishment, nor is it continued until the child is tired. The first work period is usually not longer than twelve minutes, and some children tire and are excused at seven minutes. Interest is built up by showing the children examples of grown people enjoying their work. The work atmosphere of school and home has a most powerful effect on the child and greatly affects his emotional attitude toward work. If the child sees that his mother cleans the apartment only when they are expecting guests, or shows no interest in her work, the child is unconsciously developing sloppy work attitudes.

Nechaeva found that constant reminders by the teacher to "wash your hands," to "put away your toys," and to "come and eat lunch," instead of resulting in better-behaved children, had the opposite effect. When the only comment was "It is time to have lunch," the children of their own accord, put away their toys, washed their hands and came to the luncheon table.

This self-discipline was evident in all the kindergartens we visited. The teacher seemed to be a quiet reminder in the background rather than a drill sergeant. A teacher gently dislodged an elbow from a table here or straightened a small back in a chair, but there was no shouting of commands or pleas for order and quiet. There was just order and quiet. The teachers seem to believe in the ability of the children, and the children do not disappoint the teachers.

We had lunch in many kindergartens, sitting at the little tables with the children. There were usually four of us to a table —my husband at one table with three children, and I at another table with three children.

We were told that capricious eaters were seated next to good eaters and that children who did not eat well were sometimes literally just "fed up" with a certain food, in which case that food would be discontinued or masked with a sauce of a better-liked food.

The child who fails to put his chair back or do something else that is expected of him is told, "I thought you were a big boy and could do things for yourself without being told. Perhaps you had better go back into the younger group."

The older children have a regular duty (*dezhurstvo*) to perform. *Dezhurstvo,* a systematic work activity, does not require great physical strength, but the older children have more complex demands made on them than the younger ones. *Dezhurstvo* requires the *dezhurny* to set and clear the table, care for animals and plants, put toys away, clean tables after art lessons, and do other socially useful labor for the good of the collective. The child has regular days to be on duty, and he must fulfill certain specified tasks. He knows clearly what his responsibilities are and how to fulfill them.

One American authority on Russia told me of an experience he had as a child when he attended a Russian camp and had the *dezhurstvo* job of setting the table. Among the silverware was one spoon with a round bowl instead of the usual oval shape of the other spoons. The Soviet children particularly valued this round-bowled spoon, and the child who found it at his place was particularly happy and envied by the other children that day. The American child, although he did not know why the Soviet children valued this particular spoon, was influenced by the group feeling and he too wanted the spoon.

When it was his turn to be *dezhurny* he realized that it was within his power to keep the round-bowled spoon himself or allot it to another child. He was about to put the spoon at his own place, when he noticed a Soviet child watching him. What had the Soviet children on *dezhurstvo* done with the spoon? Had they taken it themselves? He couldn't remember. The Soviet child was still watching him. He felt uncomfortable. Are American children more selfish than Soviet children, he wondered. Suddenly he put the spoon at someone else's place, determined to watch in the following days to see whether the Soviet *dezhurnyi* kept the round-bowled spoon or gave it to someone else.

For the rest of the time he was in the camp no *dezhurny* kept the spoon himself, and even though the American child watched them carefully he never knew whether or not it was hard for them to decide to give the spoon to someone else. Now, years later, he is still wondering.

Every nursery-school–kindergarten has its nature corner, where there is an aquarium with fish, plants, and flowers in pots, and perhaps a squirrel in a cage, or some other pet. These plants and animals must be taken care of, as well as the garden outside.

One teacher showing the children how to spade the garden, gave them explicit directions, as to how to hold the spade and how deep to dig, but the first results were not perfect—Vitya held the spade with one hand; Ulya did not put his foot on the

At all stages, the children are taught the social importance of labor. This little girl (above) has just finished bringing in the dirty dinner dishes. Setting the table for lunch is also "socially useful labor" required for all Soviet students. This preschooler in Kishinev (below) is on duty (dezhurny) and is responsible for assisting the adults in feeding her comrades. To be dezhurny is a high honor, much sought after by the children.

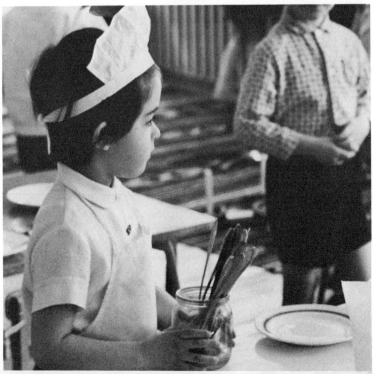

spade; Sasha held the spade backward; Nadya in trying to be first got such a big piece of dirt on her spade that she could not lift it. The teacher had to explain the whole process again, and this time the children got better results.

The children are very fond of feeding the birds or other animals and fish, and they enjoy cleaning the cages and playing with the birds. They like to help in the yard, but sometimes work turns into play, as when Natasha and Lenochka were raking leaves. They gathered a basketful and then started playing store with the leaves, which suddenly turned from leaves into cabbages and carrots and candy. In cases like this the teacher must tactfully put the children back on the work track, since the object is to teach the children to finish each task to the end.

Work in the nature corner and garden not only teaches love of nature but strengthens the child's powers of observation. The children of one kindergarten in Velikie Luki had their observations about their garden recorded in a special notebook, and one of the teachers sent her account of the garden to the magazine *Doshkolnoye Vospitanie:*

May 24: Cucumber seeds sown in beds. The children observed that the seeds were not large, with white shoots. Every child planted a seed in the row. Olya and Galya covered the seeds with dirt. Lesha watered the row. The children talked about when the seeds would germinate.

May 30: Today the girls noticed the first sprouts. They called all the other children, who saw that some of the sprouts already had two leaves. The teacher suggested that Ala and Lena water the plants.

June 5: After activities in the kindergarten all the children went with the teacher to the vegetable garden. The teacher showed them the third leaves of the cucumber plant, which were different in form from the first two leaves. They all looked at the leaves, noticing that the surface of the leaves was rough and uneven. Again, they watered the row.

June 15: The cucumbers have grown noticeably, with runners making their first appearance. During a cold spell growth slowed down. After a rain the teacher fertilized the cucumbers, explaining to the children, "Now after I feed the cucumbers, watch how they will grow."

June 23: Today the children noticed that all the plants had become green. The cucumbers were growing well. The children discovered yellow flowers on the vines.

July 5: Everyone went to the garden to see the first cucumbers. They were still very small. Two cucumbers were reserved for fall, so that seeds could be taken from them for the next planting.

July 20: Today everyone was satisfied that the cucumbers had grown noticeably.

August 8: Today is the day to harvest the cucumbers. The children watched while the teacher picked the cucumbers carefully, so as not to injure them. All the children were given cucumbers. The very first cucumbers had become yellow and were left to ripen for seed.

August 26: Picked the last two cucumbers, whose skin had become golden and cracked. They were put in a window to ripen.

August 30: Cut open the cucumbers, and the children saw the white seeds which they would put in a safe place for the winter, so that next spring they could again plant their own cucumbers.

After some detailed observations like these, the older children learn to calculate how many radishes to plant—"It takes two rows of radishes to entertain one group of guests"—and when to feed and water their plants.

Most of the house plants are rather hardy, since leaves that are constantly washed by little hands must be of the wash-and-wear variety like Amarillis, Montstera, Clivia, and palms.

Outside is the garden and the berry patches and fruit gardens; the produce from these is eaten with great pride, and mushrooms are gathered during walks in the woods and brought back to the cook.

The animal corner has chickens, hedgehogs, rabbits, turtles, birds, squirrels, and various other animate beings. One school had a parrot all the children loved. The *dezhurny* was told just how much the parrot should be fed, and he carefully measured out two teaspoonfuls of grain and two drops of fish oil twice a day.

When it was Vova's turn to feed the parrot, he carelessly gave the parrot too much fish oil. Right after that the parrot looked sick.

"What is the matter with our bird?" the children asked anxiously.

"I wanted to give him just two drops of oil," Vova said miserably, "but more spilled out."

"If you don't know how to do something, ask someone else," the children said, reminding Vova that the very life of their pet depended on how he was fed.

Fortunately, the parrot recovered, and Natasha said happily, "Today the parrot is merry. He sings all the time and jumps around all day." And, charitably, she added, "And he doesn't blame anybody but loves everybody."

From time to time, the children have group discussions about their work, telling what they have done, why they did something and how they did it, as well as their observations on the plants and animals. Frequently the parents are invited to see the Nature Corner and the progress the plants and livestock have made during the year.

Once a month all the children work together during the Sanitary Day, when the Nature Corner gets a thorough cleaning. The children forget their differences in their work toward a common goal, though the teacher has to watch for errors in judgment such as filling a pan to the very top with water and then running with it, or transferring the fish from one aquarium to the other, with too much intermittent handling of the fish.

In the summer, plants and livestock are packed up to go with the children to the *dacha* (summer home) in the country, or if the children do not go to the country, indoor plants are put outside in the sun and air. The child's initial desire just to "be good" is now translated into a more precise formula of work.

The grownups of the Soviet Union are still sentimental about the children's work. A typical story that appeals to them is the story about "Worker's Hands":

"Mama" Valerka asked, "Why is it that I can play all right, but when I try to work nothing happens?"

"It's because you have hands that are still small and not worker's hands," Valerka's mother said, smiling.

Socially useful labor is emphasized in this poster about the Octobrists. Lenin's grandchildren will graduate to Octobrists and then become Pioneers. The poster reads:

Octobrists—Future Pioneers

Only those who love work are called Octobrists.
Octobrists—pleasant children love school, respect old people.
Octobrists—truthful and brave, agile and smart.
Octobrists—friendly children.
Read and write, play and sing. Live merrily.

Valerka thought about this a minute then ran off to discuss it with other children.

"I know why we don't work like grownups do," Valerka said. "You see what small palms we have—not worker's hands."

The children compared their hands, and all agreed that they were quite small. Suddenly one child had an idea.

"Let's ask Grandfather Stepan. He is a worker and he has hands. We can see for ourselves what kind."

Grandfather Stepan considered the children's questions very seriously. "You are quite correct," he said. "Workers must have hands that can work quickly. But this work must be not for yourself alone but socially useful labor. Try and see. Every time you do something for someone else your hands will become more like workers' hands."

That night Valerka cleaned his brother's shoes and, on his own initiative, helped his mother fix the meat for the cutlets. The next morning the children cleaned the trash out of the courtyard. The parents wondered what had happened. After a few days of helping others, the children met Grandfather Stepan and showed him their hands.

Grandfather Stepan studied them. "Good fellows," he said. "You have made a beginning. Your hands are already a little stronger, but only a little. To become real workers' hands, you need to do a great deal more useful labor."

In learning about work the children also learn about their own city and country and at the same time learn about Communism. A typical schedule is that of the kindergarten on Sadovo-Chernogryazskoi Street in Moscow. On one side of the school is Lermontov Square, and on the other Karl Marx Street. The children start their acquaintance with their town through their own street. Their street got its name from the stream Chernogryazski ("Black Mud"), which used to flow through the area but is now piped underground through the efforts of Soviet workmen. *Sad* is the Russian word for "garden," so the street's name explains that what used to be a dirty stream is now a gardenlike street.

Socially Useful Labor

Since Sadovo-Chernogryazskoi Street is short, the children can soon cover it from beginning to end. On Karl Marx Street there is the interesting house that was once occupied by V. L. Pushkin, the grandfather of the great Russian poet A. S. Pushkin, who is still the favorite Soviet author. Pushkin often visited his grandfather at this house; he was born just a short distance away, on Baumana Street (formerly called German Street), but the house where Pushkin was born is not standing now. In its place is a school, named for the poet.

Lermontov Square, named for another great Russian writer and poet, was an earth rampart in the middle of the seventeenth century. On the occasion of the Russian victory over the Swedes a breach was built of wood, and then stone gates were built and called the Triumphal Gates, later Krasny ("Red") Gates, since through them traffic moved to the center of the village of Krasnoye Selo ("Red Village"). On the anniversary of the death of Lermontov, the Square of the Red Gates was renamed Lermontov Square. On the site where once stood the small house in which Lermontov was born in 1814 there is a monument to Lermontov. When the children visit the square they are shown a portrait of Lermontov and listen to a reading of his poems.

After learning about the names and history of the streets around them, the children become acquainted with the everyday activities on their street—a bakery, a grocery store, a bookstore, an eye hospital, a movie theater. As they look into the stores and hospital and movie, they see how some of the Soviet citizens work. Also on their street is the Ministry of Communication, where many people work. This ministry decides where to build new railway lines and where to put stations. It also draws up schedules for the train movements.

The children observe the traffic on their street—the bus, the trolley and the automobiles. They learn to distinguish the busstop signs and learn where to cross the street.

They are told that life for the inhabitants of Moscow was not always as favorable as it is now, under Communism. They are told stories of Tsarist days, and they visit the Museum of the History and Reconstruction of Moscow, where they see pictures of Red Square in the second half of the seventeenth century. Since all the children have been to Red Square both with their parents and with their class, they regard the old picture with interest.

"That's a picture of old Red Square," the children say.

"And how did you guess that?" the teacher asks.

"Because the people are wearing old-fashioned clothes. And instead of stars on the Kremlin tower there is the two-headed eagle."

The children look at models of old Moscow and the teacher tells them that in old Moscow the work was done by hand, that it was hard, that the city was lighted by gas lamps and only in the center of town. They see how the people traveled in sleds and carriages in days when there were no buses or automobiles. They see models of workers' houses where many families were crowded together in unsanitary buildings.

For several days after the visit to the museum, the children talk about the differences between Tsarist Moscow and Moscow since the Revolution. On their daily walks near the school they watch a new building going up. It is a new apartment house, which will have a café on its ground floor. The children notice what each worker does as his part of the building—electrician, plumber, metalworker, carpenter. They also notice the machines that help the workers—cranes and shovels. Both men and machines know their jobs, and together they work in friendly fashion. When the building is finished the children are delighted to find that the café on the ground floor sells ice cream. Two of the teachers move into apartments in the building, and the children feel they have almost had a part in building the apartments themselves.

Dr. N. A. Vetlugina, Director of the Laboratory of Esthetic Education of Moscow's Preschool Institute, examines a toy used in teaching very young children music appreciation.

·VIII·
How to Listen to Music

"HERE WE STUDY the interrelations of aesthetic education with the development of character," Dr. N. A. Vetlugina said, as we sat in her office, the Laboratory of Aesthetic Education of the Preschool Institute, surrounded by sets of bells, musical scales and musical toys. Musical education is one of the first concerns of the preschool institution.

"Children begin to respond to music at a very early age," she said. "The baby becomes aware of sound shortly after birth and soon develops a feeling of rhythm and tempo, and this gives him pleasure. In developing a multisided personality, we are very much interested in enriching the spiritual world of the child and in encouraging his creativity. We believe there is a close connection between instruction and creativity, so we start teaching him at an early age."

She picked up a box that had three dolls affixed to the top, and after studying the dolls a minute, she touched the first one, which was dressed in Uzbekian costume. The doll turned in place and the box began to play an Uzbekian tune. Dr. Vetlugina listened in delight, then touched the other two dolls, which emitted a Russian melody and a Moldavian song to match their respective costumes.

"For two-year-olds we have these," she said, picking up another box, with a cow on the top. When the lid was opened the cow said *"Mo-o-o-o."* Another box, with a cat on it said, *"Miaow."* Her face beamed like a two-year-old's.

"Instruction shows the child how to develop his abilities and makes it possible for him to teach himself, express himself and control himself. Through creativity the world opens to him and he to the world."

Vetlugina, in discussing her department, told us about the plans for developing a well-rounded personality through aesthetic education.

Vetlugina is very much concerned with the problem of creativity, which she defines as the ability of the child to do something new. Teaching creativity is not a simple matter. Vetlugina believes that the teacher must start with the basic nature of the child and build his creative ability from the child's natural love of activity. As in all education, aesthetic education must be closely connected with the day-to-day experience of the child, helping him to perceive, feel and understand the beauty in his everyday life. Teaching must not be a brake on creativity, but must show the child his potential for creativity.

Aesthetic education begins with sensory perception, chiefly the perception of sight and sound. At first the child is attracted to bright-colored objects, such as the beads hanging over his crib, and it is objects such as these that he will first describe as "pretty." Even though he is but dimly aware of them, the color of the hospital and nursery-school walls, the furniture and plants around the room help to introduce the child to beauty. At early ages, the child uses "pretty" to describe objects, colors and animals, but seldom people; and it is only toward the age of five or six that the child can associate "pretty" with nature.

Because the young child responds to music more than to any other artistic form, his musical education may begin in the first few months of his life. He has heard sounds from birth, but these sounds mean little to him. Gradually, he associates the voices of the people around him with the pleasure of eating, and his first smile is usually a response to a talking, smiling adult. At home, he hears the sounds of the radio and television, and his mother often hums a lullaby as she cuddles him in her arms. If he goes to *yasli* at two or three months of age, he is sung to and talked to, so that by the time he is three or four months of age he can distinguish various sounds sufficiently to turn his head in the direction of the sound.

The *yasli*'s musical goals for the child's first year of life are to develop emotional responsiveness to music, to strengthen his ability to hear and listen to music attentively, and the ability to remember certain movements connected with the music. Even little babies learn to clap their hands when someone sings "Ladushki."

The child should learn to love music and to listen to it attentively. The baby not only hears music in the background at the *yasli*, but at six or seven months he is also given exercises in individual listening, which is vital to musical appreciation.

The teacher approaches the child playing a mirliton or sometimes simply humming tenderly. When the child shows that he is listening to the music (by turning his head toward the sounds) the teacher moves the child's hands and legs in a passive little "dance." There must be no other diverting sounds or movements in the room when the child first listens to music, and without distractions the very young child can listen attentively for two or three minutes at a time. This is not only the beginning of musical education but also the first lesson in concentration, which the child will need in his later educational work.

In the play dance, the teacher moves the child's limbs in rhythm with the music. Slow, peaceful movements in the music bring correspondingly quiet physical movements, while lively, gay music brings more active movements of the arms and legs. After the child has had individual attention with manipulated movement during a musical interlude, he may listen to the same song, in a group, without individual attention.

After the child is six or seven months old, he listens in a group to music in which the slow and lively parts are more clearly differentiated. The duration of the two parts should not be more than five minutes, during which time the "musician" moves about the room and waves a flag or shakes a tambourine to attract the child's attention.

At six or seven months of age, the child is also shown the musical instrument itself before the music begins. This teaches him to recognize various musical instruments and gives him a signal to adjust himself for listening. Now the musician is active during the lively parts of the music but stands still during the slow parts.

When the majority of the children are able to sit up by themselves (which greatly increases their field of vision) the adult, while playing, suddenly disappears from view for a few seconds and stops playing the music. After a short pause she starts playing again and reappears. At the end of the "concert" the teacher hits the tambourine with the palm of her hand and then gives it to the children to hit. The "more emotional" children are delighted and laugh aloud as they hit the tambourine.

As the children become more experienced, the dance part of the music can last as long as six or seven minutes, with the whole performance taking twelve to fifteen minutes. The children now begin to take an active interest in the teacher's individual play with the other children and wave their arms about as the teacher moves one child's arms in time with the music. The children soon learn to listen to the quiet part of the music without movement.

When manipulating the dance with one child, if the teacher notices that the child next to him seems interested, she may join the children's hands, and occasionally lets three children join hands in their first "group dance." The children are now interested in watching the teacher approach another child singing "Here Comes the Horned Goat," and they laugh appreciatively at the other child's response.

The child from seven months to a year old can hit the tambourine himself, clap his hands for "Ladushki" and conform to the rhythm of the music by "dancing" during the lively parts and being quiet during the peaceful parts. Now he can imitate the intonation of a grownup's voice, with a joyful *"Aha-a-a"* in the game of "Hide" or an *"Ai"* in the musical game of "Birds."

At one and a half, the child begins to respond to words. Now the teacher, before starting the music lesson, shows the child the musical instrument and says, *"Muzika* [Music]?" The teacher plays a peaceful melody for fifteen or twenty seconds, then stops playing and places the instrument on the floor or a chair, and covers it up with a cloth.

"Nyet muzika," she says, emphasizing the word *"nyet"* by dropping her hands to her side.

"Where is the music?" she asks next. A child runs to the place the musical instrument is hiding and the teacher takes the cloth off with a flourish.

"A vot muzika [Here is the music]!" she says, and she starts to play again. This little byplay keeps the children's attention and shows them the meaning of the word *nyet* ("no") in a painless way.

These musical activities strengthen the child's group identity and develop mental powers of comparison and association in differentiating the tempo of the music. He is learning the meaning of words, and he listens carefully while the teacher explains the words of a song.

For some time the children have been rocking their dolls while the teacher hums; and in the song about a cat, they can call the cat with a *"ks-ks-ks"* or bark *"av-av"* (Russian for "bow-wow") when the dog appears in the song. At this age, sound impressions are still more stimulating to the child than sight impressions.

Although the child of one and a half watches attentively when the teacher dances or plays with one of his comrades, he usually expresses no desire to participate, and even actively rejects such suggestions when offered to him. Individual play with the teacher is more important to him than group play, though the whole group listens to music for seven or eight minutes before receiving individual attention. At the teacher's command, the child can dance by himself, run in place or jump on one leg.

From one and a half to two years of age, the children are beginning simple role-playing games like "Mouse and Children," "Birds," and other games which coordinate speech with the music. Before the music starts, the teacher explains briefly and clearly what the children are to look for in the song.

A lesson in listening. The teacher sings and beats time; the children respond. The child learns by participating in group socialization and develops mental powers of comparison, differentiating between notes or tempos. He learns to listen carefully and increases his vocabulary as the teacher explains the songs.

If the song is to be Tchaikovsky's "Song of the Lark," the teacher says, "Have you heard how the birds sing in the summer? Their song is beautiful and clear. The lark is such a bird singer. It sings especially well and flies easily and swiftly. Listen to the lark in this song."

In the song games the children listen for the teacher's instructions—"The children sit down to rest"; or, "The children begin to dance." They run when they hear the dog "bark" in the song, or jump like the rabbit or walk like the bear. Now they begin to dance with one another as well as with the teacher, though if a child objects to dancing with another child, he is not pushed into it. The teacher is careful to note the "passive" children, so she can give them individual attention to draw them out. The goal is for each child to become an active member of the collective.

At two, the children are starting to dance freely with one another and they can sing lullabies to their dolls. They begin to coordinate their behavior to outward signals of sight and sound. Now the child is very active. From one second to another he sits down, stands up, and walks again, habitually busy, usually with some toy in his hand. He finds it difficult to hold one position for long and tires quickly of one form of movement.

By his third year, the child has usually mastered many complex movements and is beginning to orient himself to words. When asked how he knows the song is about a rabbit, he will say, "Because it's like a rabbit and because I am big." When he really is big (five or six) he will say, "I know it is a rabbit from the music—for a bear the music is rough, for a rabbit it is merry."

Vetlugina's department has invented all sorts of contraptions to help the preschool child learn music. There is a set of little bells mounted on wires set into a board. When tapped the bells sound the scales. There are also little sets of steps with a note of the scale on each step. The Russian wooden doll Matreshka climbs the steps, and as she climbs she plays "*Do-re-mi-fa-so-la-ti-do.*" The children learn the difficult differentiation between high and low notes by watching and listening to Matreshka. She is standing on the "*la*" step now. Is that higher or lower than the "*do*" step? The treads to the steps can be changed from major to minor.

The children are asked to sing their own names, using an appropriate note for each syllable.

By three the children have strengthened their powers of observation so that they can correct mistakes of pronunciation or steps in some other child's song or dance, even while making the same mistakes themselves. They know the rules of listening. The older children may also volunteer, or be elected, to take an active part in a musical game involving a mouse or a rabbit or a bear.

"Now who would make a good Mishka?" the teacher asks, and the children are usually ready with a choice. Kolya, of course. Kolya looks very happy, as he has a bear's cap tied on his head, and it is hard to say whether Kolya or his audience is more pleased. Vicarious pleasure is fun too, and teachers and children admire each other extravagantly, seemingly never tiring of watching each other perform.

Sometimes the teacher says she is going to play what happens in the forest (or in the courtyard, or on the street) and the children listen to the story the music tells. A rabbit hops along in the forest, is suddenly frightened and tries to hide. What has frightened him? *Clump, clump, clump.* Here is Mishka the bear.

Before the song *"Dozhdik* [Rain]," the teacher asks the children to try to remember how raindrops sound when they fall and to see if the composer made the rain sound the way it should. Musical appreciation begins to develop into musical criticism. Analysis and synthesis lead to logical thinking.

The teacher must "mobilize" the children's hearing. To do this she must pick the best time, which is at the beginning of activity periods, when their hearing is fresh and they are able to sit quietly. Humorous songs delight the child's burgeoning sense of humor.

When the children hear a musical picture of the courtyard they imitate the ducks, chickens, birds, kittens and other animals they hear in the music. They hear the rooster walking in his pompous, leisurely way, and they lift their feet high as they march around the room, imitating the way the rooster walks, as the teacher says, "Here comes the rooster, proudly lifting his head with the red comb, lifting high his legs with spurs."

The older children are expected to be able to classify the music. Is it a march, a dance or a lullaby? Is the tempo fast or slow? Is it loud or soft? Does it have high notes or low notes? Can they recognize the song, without the words?

By the time they are five or six, the children will be asked to sing songs in answer to a question, such as "What does the bear do?"

"Khodit, bro-dit, po lu-gu [Walks and roams through the meadow]" is the musical answer, now recorded on a tape recorder and played back for all the children to hear. When one child gets too high, everyone laughs and the child sings in a

Kindergarten children in each of the 15 Soviet republics are taught the traditions of their particular republic. This young man in native costume recites in an Ashkabad kindergarten against a typical Turkmenian background. Ashkabad, Turkmenia, USSR (1969).

lower key, on the next tape. They draw the musical notes in their *tetrad* ("notebook").

Each of the many nationalities in the Soviet Union has its own native songs and dances, and the children are encouraged to sing and dance them. A Moldavian learns native dances quite different from those of a Turkmenian child. Old Russian folk songs are often sung in kindergarten too, though they do present problems today, since the customs sung about belong to a past that modern children often do not understand. The old folk songs frequently have such endless variations of story that it is often confusing to the children, and to the teacher too, who must choose the correct version for her class.

Some native songs seem to come naturally to the children. "Rabbit You, Rabbit," "Soroka, Soroka", and "Here Comes the Horned Goat" are all popular, as are "Guli, Guli, Gulenki" and "Solnishko."

An album of music for children made by Tchaikovsky is very popular, and the children also like Rimsky-Korsakov, Grieg, Schumann, Schubert and others. Sometimes foreign visitors to the schools are startled to hear Bach or Mozart played on an accordion or some other composition played on native instruments like the four-stringed dombra or the flute-like sopilla.

The children love to play in an orchestra, with or without instruments. Most of the children want to be the orchestra leader, so the teacher must tactfully influence the choice. The soloist is also a popular role. The favorite songs are not children's songs, but grownups' songs; "An Evening near Moscow" was chosen for one "soloist" for her performance.

Some Soviet teachers are criticized for being satisfied with their pupils' singing when the children know the words, no matter how badly they sing the tune. These critics are interested in the connection between the child's hearing and his voice, and they feel that the nerve centers connected with hearing have a close connection with the centers of thought in the brain.

The child who does not hear well has trouble with correct intonation, and defective hearing is also one cause of bad singing, since the child cannot coordinate his voice with the sound he hears. Sometimes a new song pleases a child instantly and he wants to hear it again, but other songs do not please him until he knows more about them. In the second case the teacher tries to give the child a goal in listening—"Do you think you can remember this melody?" or, "The child who knows this song best can sing it on International Women's Day."

The teacher also asks the children to listen carefully and tell her where the high notes are in the song and where the low notes are. "What words do we sing to the highest notes?" "How do we make the sounds last longer?"

The children can also learn to form musical judgments, but the educators stress that music is a pleasure, not a school exercise. So music lessons are not full of restrictions, even though the children are asked to sit deeply in their chairs, holding themselves straight, with both feet firmly on the floor. Sitting properly, a three-year-old can safely sing in the range of *mi-la*; a four- or five-year-old, *re-ti*; a six-year-old, *re-do*.

To sing well, the child should have the proper inner feelings for the song he is to sing. If he is to sing a lullaby, he must feel tenderness and compassion for the doll or child to whom he is singing. For a march, he must feel the joy of life.

His singing diction must be clear and correct. The teacher, as always, must be a good example. Usually she sings the song first, and then the children are asked to sing it. They are shown the high and low notes with gestures of the hand and soon learn to follow the teacher's direction and sing simple short songs in clear tones.

As with most learning in *yasli* and *detsky sad,* there are many games to teach music. There are games in which the children sing loudly or softly to match the words of the song. These games demand that the child listen attentively to the music and respond with some physical action, like clapping the hands in "Ladushki" and "Kulachki," or competitive running in games like "The Hunters and the Rabbits."

In the latter game the hunters move forward during the first and third couplets of the music, their song and movements clear-cut and decisive. In the second and fourth couplets they are looking for the rabbits and their movements are searching. The rabbits sing very softly so the hunters won't find them, and their movements are very quiet until they actually come close to the hunters. Then in a loud voice the rabbits say defiantly, "Catch us!" and run away as fast as they can, with the hunters after them.

There are other games, in which the child turns his back as the teacher plays some musical instrument ("Guess what I am playing.") or imitates a bird or animal ("Guess who it is.") or plays a tune suggesting some activity ("Guess whose house this is."). Others take the form of a chorus of voices with which the children present a musical picture, as in the composition "The Children and the Baby Elephant." As the other children sing a light melody, *"Lya, lya, lya,"* two children representing the elephant, dance, singing *"Dzha-bum, dzha-bum, dzha-bum."*

The games all have rules, which must be followed. These rules help to define the music too—"Did you represent this sound correctly?"—and help correct reproduction of sounds— "How did you make this sound?" The game must meet aesthetic demands, awaken the emotions of the children and lead to expressive movements.

Differentiation of sounds is practiced in the game "Our Orchestra," in which children take the parts of musical instruments and play in unison, with the drum pounding out its Russian name, *"Bar-a-ban, bar-a-ban,"* as the other "instruments" join in.

"Musical Lotto" is a favorite game, in which tunes and pictures are matched on a card. There is also "Note Lotto," in which a note is played and the child places a cardboard note on the proper line of the wooden staff before him. By this time, the children know that there are short sounds and long sounds, and that the long sign is represented by a black circle with a stick on the end of it and a short sound is described by a black circle with a stick that has a tail on it. After the children have all the notes placed on their lines, they sing the song they have made.

The children love to study musical A-B-C's, and Vetlugina has written an attractive book for children and their parents, with the left-hand pages for the parents and the right-hand pages for the children. Toward the end of the book the children are invited to "sing by note."

One of the objects of kindergarten is to teach children how to think, so the musical lessons proceed to new situations, wherein the child must improvise on an unknown musical instrument. In one experiment all the children in the class except Zoya were introduced to the new instruments. They sat at the upright piano and fingered the keys, after which they were given a restricted area (first octave) of the keyboard in which to play.

After a week, it was suggested that the children play again, and this time their attention was called to the fact that they could play their own new tunes. While Zoya also had composed tunes, she used the habits she had learned from *forte-piano* play and simply played a familiar exercise—arpeggio. She played *"do"* with the first finger, *"mi"* with the third, and *"sol"* with the fifth. Marina's creation was extremely modest; she did not copy a known piece, but created her own, building on fragments from pieces she knew.

"Quietly, in the forest . . . the birds sing." Marina fingered the keys in the upper register. "And suddenly . . . a wolf. No, first, it's better a rabbit. . . . And this butterfly dances." She fingered the keys in something resembling a waltz, then stood up and began to dance, imitating the flight of the butterfly.

Performing for Mama (or anyone who happens by) is one of the pleasures of all kindergarten children in the Soviet Union. The children can put on a complete program with perfect aplomb at any given moment, and their delight in their performance and their friends' performances is so great that even foreign photographers' flash bulbs do not distract them from their performances.

Holidays always call for special programs. Some time before a holiday the parents, teachers and children begin preparations. The parents help with costumes and decorations, and the children learn dances, songs and recitations. The program is planned so that the liveliest numbers come in the second half of the program, when the children's attention might otherwise wander.

Music plays a big part in the four main holiday occasions during the year—October Revolution Day on November 7; New Year's Day when Ded Moroz (Grandfather Frost) and the Snow Maiden come with presents; International Woman's Day on March 8; and International Worker's Day on the first of May.

One of the favorite holidays is International Woman's Day, which is like our Mother's Day. The children practice songs and dances and speeches for weeks ahead of time, as they make presents for Mama and Grandmother in honor of Woman's Day.

The children particularly love to present the musical picture "The Children and the Baby Elephant," because the elephant's costume is so real. A narrow rubber hose is inserted in the elephant's papier-mâché trunk, with a rubber syringe filled with water at the end. When the trunk is squeezed, water comes out of the trunk to the amazement of everyone, as the children sing, *"Dzha-bum, dzha-bum."*

The music for the dance of the rabbits suggested movement to the teacher, but one group of five-year-olds, practicing the dance, kept dancing in one place until the teacher said, "If you rabbits keep on dancing in one place, there will be a deep hole in the snow. The tracks of the rabbits must be seen everywhere."

The songs are usually the distinguishing feature between one holiday "matinee" and another. For Mother there are special songs:

> *Mama, mama,* mamushka
> *I love you.*
> *I sing you*
> *A merry song.*

and another, called "My Mama," which begins,

> *If the sun wakes up*
> *The morning begins to shine,*
> *If Mama smiles*
> *How joyful the day becomes!*
> *How joyful the day becomes!*

No matter what the holiday, two songs are always sung: "Moya Rodina [My Motherland]" and "There Will Always be Mama."

> *May there always be Mama*
> *May there always be me.*

·IX·

The Techniques of Beauty

AN AMERICAN EDUCATOR I know once watched an art class in the Soviet Union. There were twenty children in the class, and at the end of the period there were twenty absolutely identical drawings. He concluded that Soviet art was completely regimented, just as he had expected it to be.

He watched only one lesson. If he had watched more than one lesson he might have seen how what appears to be regimentation can lead to the development of personal initiative. I might have concluded the same thing as my friend did, from the first art lesson I watched.

It was in Sochi, in the spring. The teacher, a pretty young girl, started the class with a little talk: "What season of the year is this? Yes, it is spring. What happens in spring? Yes, flowers appear, but first buds come out on the branches. Today we will draw a branch."

She picked up a branch of a flowering cherry tree and tacked it on to a piece of cardboard, which she then pinned to the blackboard. There were no flowers on the branch, just buds. The small buds at the ends were still tightly closed in their green sheaths, but there were large pink buds at the bottom.

On the teacher's desk in the front of the room were two pots of paint, one of red and one of black. Beside her desk was an easel with a piece of drawing paper tacked to it. On the children's desks were similar pots of black and red paint and camel's-hair paintbrushes propped up on little blocks.

The teacher picked up her own brush, then paused. "What do we see? That's right. A branch. We will draw a branch. How

do we do it? From left to right. We will start at the bottom of the drawing paper." She dipped her brush in black paint and drew a branch across the sheet of paper.

"Now we have a branch. What have we left out? Buds. We will draw the buds with red paint." The teacher drew a branch and put buds on it. "We start with the little buds at the top of the branch." The children watched as the teacher finished her drawing. Then she asked them to get ready to paint. This was the signal for the children to pull their chairs closer to the table and to correct their posture. They started to paint, following her example, dipping their brushes into the little jars of water and then into the pots of paint.

The teacher guided the hand of one little boy who seemed uncertain how to begin. She moved another child's left hand from the top of the paper to the upper left-hand corner. He accepted the move without complaint, but moved his hand back to the old position as soon as the teacher left. The teacher talked in a soft, soothing voice, like a mother cat purring to her kittens. Twenty little hands drew branches from left to right, and soon there were fifteen branches resembling the teacher's drawing. Five children were still working.

The teacher held up a picture one child had finished. "Do you like Tanya's picture? Why do you like it?" Five hands were raised from the elbow, the elbow supported by the palm of the right hand in the approved Soviet way. The teacher nodded to Ludmila, who stood up stiffly by her desk.

"I think Tanya has fulfilled her plan very well," Ludmila said. "I like her branch because it looks like spring. Her buds are very clear and red."

A few more paintings were discussed. Then those children who had finished went into the next room to wash their hands. Two girls on *dezhurstvo* began vigorously scrubbing and wiping the tables, while three children continued to paint. They did not seem to feel hurried or pressed. When they were finished, they followed the others to the washroom and then dressed for an outdoor walk.

The uniformity of the paintings depends on the teacher, the ability of the pupils and the goal. The children must learn the mechanics of drawing before they can be original, just as it

is necessary to know the alphabet before writing words. The Soviets want a firm foundation for imagination.

Although the younger children are urged to paint representational pictures, their works often look abstract, due more to inability than recalcitrance. Vygotsky said that the very small child draws something first, then names what he has drawn. When he is older he will name the drawing when it is half drawn, and when he is much older he can decide beforehand what he will draw. The Sochi children we saw were about five, old enough to be given a specific goal.

In the past the official Soviet attitude toward art has been blunt and unequivocal: "We do not like abstract art for the simple reason that abstract art takes us away from reality, from labor and beauty, from joy and sorrow, from the very throb of life, into an illusory and spectral world, into the futility of so-called self-expression." This statement occurs in the book *Questions and Answers,* intended by the Soviets to explain their country to English-speaking foreigners.

At the Institute of Artistic Education in Moscow, the people we talked to were not as adamant about representational art. Some abstract art, they said, is now part of art history and should be taught, even if not encouraged. In their studies they found that children through elementary school prefer representational art, and that it is only older children who like abstract art. Now children interested in art history may, in the seventh to ninth grades, take an optional course that includes abstract art as well as religious art, which is taught as art, not as religion.

The attitude toward abstract art does not in any way lessen the Soviet desire for creativity in art, but the child must learn how to use his tools before he can create anything. Creativity begins with an understanding of color, form and proportion.

The Laboratory of Aesthetic Education is very much interested in what motivates aesthetic feeling in children and has done extensive experimentation on the subject. In one such experiment a group of fifty children three and four years of age were shown four pictures, which reproduced the paintings of

four Soviet artists. Two were bright, decorative and conventional in the manner of folk art, but clearly based on reality—one of a simple earthenware pot with flowers, the other a bouquet of slightly more complicated pattern. The other two paintings were vague and more abstract, though also of flowers, but with many more flowers than the first two paintings contained, as well as other distracting details.

The children were asked to select the prettiest picture from the group. Marina's reaction was typical of this first approach to the children. Marina smoothed her dress over her knees, as she glanced quickly at the pictures, but she did not answer the teacher's question.

Teacher: "Marina, I asked you to choose the prettiest picture."

Marina (looking out the window): "It's snowing." (She pulled at her slippers, touched her face, glanced at her fingers.)

Teacher: "Marina, look how many different pictures. Well, choose the prettiest."

Marina (seizing one picture from the table and giving it to the teacher): "For you, for you, for you. That's all." (She started for the door).

So many of the children seemed to have no conception of what choosing the prettiest meant that the educators were inclined to think that the task had been presented to the children at too early an age. Feeling that emotional factors might play a part, the experimenters tried a new task. This time the children were asked to take the prettiest picture to their mothers.

The change in the question resulted in an unexpected change in the response of the children. Now eighty-four percent of the children approached the task with great interest. When asked "Why do you want this for your mother?" or "What is pretty here?" the children showed surprisingly good judgment in elementary aesthetic feelings. They selected color, color combination and form as elements of beauty. Lena's reaction was typical now:

Lena (animatedly, sorting the pictures): "Here are flowers. Here's an earthenware pot, flowers, bouquet. Here is the prettiest, because it is smeared with paint." She had chosen the simple picture of the earthenware pot with flowers. Her answer "smeared with paint" meant that she was attracted by the clear, bright colors of the painting. The majority of the children agreed with Lena's choice, showing that the children's preference followed the Soviet line of thought.

Observation is the most heavily emphasized exercise in art training. Observe, and observe again. "Check your drawing with what you see." The children learn to compare a ball with a balloon, to discover how they are alike, how they differ. On walks they are asked to watch what happens when the wind blows. They see how the grass and trees bend in the wind, so they learn to reproduce this sight in their drawings.

The Soviets, in line with their attitude toward representational art, place great emphasis on drawing from nature and from everyday life. The 1969 *Program* puts even more emphasis on the orientation of the child to his environment than did the previous programs. As the child observes, draws from observation, and checks his drawing with more observation, he is also orienting himself to his environment.

Proportion is difficult for the young child, particularly the proportion of the human body. Before the child is asked to draw a person on paper, he practices by making a snowman so he can feel the proportions of the various parts of the body, but even the most advanced kindergarten child is apt to draw a man or woman with an enormous head and short, spindly legs.

Cutting and pasting work done in an appliqué project also helps the child to get a feeling for shape. His appliqués are

Preschool attempts at realism often look abstract. (Below) Appliqué work
helps the child get a feeling for shape.

often snowmen with three round cutouts of white for head and body, with a sharp, cutout nose, and a hat pasted on the head. Rabbits are another favorite appliqué, and they resemble the snowman except that long ears are added.

One teacher suggested that the children draw a parrot, after first looking at one that was in a cage in their classroom. The children were sure that they already knew what the parrot looked like, having looked at him every day since they had entered kindergarten.

"If you have looked at him," the teacher said, "Tell me what the parrot's body most resembles?"

The children began to look at the parrot with new eyes. "A cucumber," they said. "The parrot's body is a green cucumber."

"And his beak?"

"A hook."

"And his tail?"

"Long. It hangs over."

"Does the parrot have a neck?" the teacher asked. "What color are his claws?" The teacher took a piece of paper and with quick strokes of her brush painted the parrot.

"Does this look like the parrot?"

"*Ochen* [Very]."

"Draw him yourselves, now."

The children started to paint. A fat boy painted red wings and a red beak on his cucumber body. One girl's parrot seemed to have three legs. One of the parrots had a foot with five claws, the second foot had four claws—and a third leg, which was shorter than the other two, had three clawlike fingers. Another child had painted his parrot's tail long and shaggy like a dog's. The sun was shining on some parrots with brilliant red rays, while rain was pouring on one or two. One parrot resembled a cat. There were green parrots, red parrots, and blue parrots. Was this serious work or was it play?

"Both serious work and play," said Ariadna Zhukova, a Soviet authority on children's drawings. "It was work from imagination and from nature." Then she added, "Small children can't draw accurately from nature. The teacher must teach them to draw, but first to observe and then observe again. They must also know when to stop. One child, who had drawn quite a respectable-looking parrot, then added a bright-green, froglike man.''

On their walks about town the children look out for things that they can draw, model and paint. They are taught to observe and appreciate everyday things. They might decide at one art lesson to model in clay a dog they saw in the courtyard the day before.

The teacher takes a lump of clay and says, "Now, you will model a nice, pretty dog. I will show you how to form a muzzle out of the ball of clay." She models a piece of clay. "For ears you will stretch a piece of clay into a three-cornered piece." She puts the ears on the dog as the children watch intently, murmuring, "Ears."

The children watch as she puts a neck on the dog, then attaches a body, four legs and, finally, a tail. The children examine the dog, anxious to start their own models. The children sit on their stools at the table as the teacher divides the clay among them.

"Divide your clay so that you will have one piece for the head and another for the body." The teacher says. "Then you can start."

Oleg tries several times to make a muzzle, before he is satisfied with it. Finally he has a muzzle he likes, and he attaches two pointed ears. Then he adds two small lumps of clay for eyes. Nearby, Borya draws a mouth on his dog with his fingernail, and Oleg follows his example. The children are very quiet.

Tanya forgets that she must hold the dog in one hand as she adds the legs, and one of her dog's legs cracks. The teacher warns the rest of the class of this danger. Borya, having finished his dog, rolls a long, thin piece of clay, puts it around his dog's neck, and calls it a dog collar. Then he and Tanya mold bells for their dog's collars.

"The dogs need some meat," Zhenya says.

"I don't know how to make meat," Tanya says. "I'll make a

ball for the dog to play with." Then, not sure of herself she says, "Borya, would you play with a ball?"

Borya, imitating a dog, barks, and says, "Yes, I would."

Raya comes up to the teacher with a complaint: "Tanya is teasing my dog."

"You mustn't tease the dog, Tanya," the teacher says. "It's better to feed it." Smiling, Tanya throws a little piece of clay to Raya's dog.

After about twenty minutes all the dogs are finished. The children put them on the table and wash their hands. The teacher looks at the dogs. "Let's see if all the dogs have tails and ears."

"They all have," say the children.

"What is this dog lacking?" the teacher points to one dog. The children look at the dog carefully. "She doesn't have any nose. She has a collar but no nose." It is Vitya's dog; so Vitya comes up and quickly puts a nose on his dog.

"Now everyone has a fine dog," the teacher says.

The teacher must cultivate the child's sense of beauty. Sometimes she must make the child see beauty where apparently none exists. In many of the new Soviet industrial towns there is little physical beauty to be found. After their first excursion through one such town the kindergarten children had some uncomplimentary remarks: "Nevinomissk is not very pretty, because there are few flowers." "Moscow is better than our town; there they have subways." "Our town is bad; children can't swim in our river, the Kuban."

The teacher did not contradict the children. She began by telling them about the names of the streets in Nevinomissk—Mendeleyev, Pavlova, Tchaikovsky, Gagarin. Did the children know about the people for whom these streets were named? She took them to the huge chemical plant, where most of the parents worked and told them how much the factory contributed to the glory of the Soviet Union. Finally, she showed them the town plan for the future and showed the children how they and their parents could help to make the city beautiful in fact as well as in achievement.

In the *yasli,* artistic education begins at about a year and a half with the "feel" of materials. The child plays with sand and water, and rolls clay into balls. Although the child of this age has begun to show some interest in drawing and modeling, his work is aimless. He will have no conception of formal technique until he is three, when he starts formal lessons.

At three, the child is given detailed instructions on how to hold the pencil with the fingers of his right hand, not too close to the end, point side down. He is told to "draw" only on paper or on the blackboard, not to rumple the paper, not to tap with his pencil, and to use his materials accurately, without spilling paint or clay on himself, the chair or the floor. These instructions are given quite gently but firmly. Good habits of work are the initial goals. At the end of the period all materials are put away.

The child is taught how to make certain forms on paper— a straight line, a circle, a wavy line. These beginning exercises are often done in the guise of a game. The first circles are usually imaginary ones drawn in the air, until the child's muscles are trained enough to make the same motions on paper. The teacher constantly encourages the children, and if the child is uncertain about some unrecognizable object he has made the teacher will often suggest, "Why that must be a duck." When one child pasted the legs of a cat on the top of the cat instead of the bottom part and the other children laughed at the appliqué, the teacher said, "Lena's cat has fallen down on its back. See how its legs are sticking up in the air." The teacher's comment gave the children a new point of view and showed that a work that is different is not necessarily wrong.

The art program proceeds according to the plan of the *Program,* with the yearly activities divided into quarters and with definite goals for each quarter. At three the child concentrates on straight lines, drawing them on paper in the form of ribbons, carpet strips, fences and other linear objects.

At three they learn to roll clay into a linear pattern too, and by the first quarter of their fourth year they are modeling drumsticks and sausages, and balls and rain drops. When the child has achieved a good representational result, he goes on to other objects taken from his daily life. He lines up blocks to make fences and roads.

The second quarter of the fourth year proceeds from linear shapes to round and curved forms, and the joining of the two. A curved form joined to a straight line becomes a tree. Bricks are used to build simple houses, benches and bridges.

The third quarter is occupied with color and how to use it to make green trees, red flags and other objects. By the fourth quarter the child is drawing things from his experience. He can hold the pencil confidently and is able to keep the clay off his clothes and the chair. He can name six colors— red, yellow, green, blue, black and white—and he starts using water colors as well as colored pencils.

In the fifth year the children perfect their skills in drawing, pasting, cutting, modeling and building. Now they build simple toys for themselves or their parents out of natural materials (pine cones, leaves, straw), build in the sandbox outside and with large building blocks inside.

The new program gradually introduces elements of school-work into the art program. At five the child is beginning to be able to draw something at the request of the teacher, without first being shown how to do it. Sometimes the teacher demonstrates a project and then the child is allowed to do it independently, without suggestions or corrections.

N. P. Sakulina, an authority on preschool art, took us to one of the kindergartens connected with the Preschool Institute to see an art class she was conducting. A five-year-old group was modeling roosters out of clay. Before she started, Sakulina asked the children if they knew how a rooster differed from a chicken and how chickens differed from other birds. The children discussed the rooster's distinguishing features— his big tail, his wattles and comb—before they began to model.

"We try to create creativity in the child," Sakulina said. "When he has observed specific details from life he makes better models in clay. The children are encouraged to talk about their

Young Pioneers preparing puppets for a puppet show.

work, even while they are doing it, as verbalization concretizes reality."

Sakulina pointed out the rooster that one little boy had made. The child had added three little baby chicks to the rooster's back. Both the chicks and the rooster were beautifully made. "The child is very talented," Sakulina said. "He will go to art school when he finishes primary school. We have two special art schools for talented children who have finished the three- or four-year course in the primary grades. One is a five-year course and the other a seven-year course. Both cover regular school subjects but also specialize in art. The seven-year school prepares the child for the fine-arts institutes, and the five-year school prepares him for technical school or industrial art institute or a pedagogical institute. The pedagogical institute graduate who majored in art may become an art teacher in a kindergarten."

In one experimental class the children were divided into three groups on the basis of the way they drew according to plan, their relation to the process of drawing, and their interest in the results (that is, the finished picture).

The first group, which was the smallest, consisted of children who worked on their drawings seriously but without undue hurry. These children could discuss in detail what they would draw and then draw it according to plan. Thus, Dima explained that he would draw a study of war maneuvers. Pointing to the upper part of a blank sheet of paper, he said, "In the sky is an escadrille of airplanes." He pointed to the bottom of the paper. "Here come some tanks and running alongside them are infantrymen, while in the distance trucks are bringing big guns." Dima knew exactly what he would draw and where on the paper each item belonged. His finished picture matched his plan.

The second group of children set about drawing without thinking or talking about what they would draw. They drew things they had drawn previously—a house, a three-branched tree, the girl with the big head and short spindly legs, and some stylized flowers. Every blank space on the paper was filled with dots or with paint. All of these drawings were surprisingly alike, though accurately done. Nothing new or unusual was added to any of them.

The third group, like the second group, began to draw without thinking or planning; but, unlike the second group, they proceeded in an entirely different manner. They drew quickly, energetically, hurrying to put down some idea that had just occurred to them. They had crossing lines, bright colors and no particular form to their drawings.

Typical was Galya's drawing, which showed "how we forgot to turn off the water faucet and flooded the apartment." She had started out to draw a table and chair and then began to "pour" water on everything until the whole picture was a blue mass of "flooding." Galya was enthusiastic about the process of drawing; but children are interested not only in the process but in the results. They wanted the other children to admire their drawings and understand what they were about. When the children looked at Galya's picture, all they could see was the blue paint smeared over everything. They didn't like Galya's picture, and Galya was grief-stricken.

Despite the differences in the drawings of the three groups there were also some similarities: no one used a pencil for preliminary sketches, and no one tried to correct mistakes in the pictures. They considered the blank places on the paper not as empty space that surrounds objects, but as something which must be filled in. When the teacher asked to see the finished drawings, Vanya, who had not filled in all his empty space, said, "I have to do mine over. I still have some empty spaces."

The children were very much interested in seeing the other children's drawings, but were also critical—"Not pretty" . . . "Don't understand what it is all about" . . . "Too smeared."

The Soviet experimenters concluded that much of the children's work was not thought out and that at this age the children needed more instruction. The experimenters showed the children that it was not enough just to have an idea and rush into drawing it. Such drawings would not be admired by the other children. First there must be a plan and a preliminary sketch. The drawings must proceed from the general to the specific.

Again the drawings were analyzed, but again the drawings fell into three classes. When it was suggested to the children in the second group that they add something new to their drawings they added new houses or new figures like the ones already in the drawing. The children in the third group seemed to benefit from the instruction the most. Now, instead of starting to work immediately and impulsively they paused to consider whether they could fulfill their own plans.

Next, the experimenters tried individual work with the children, correcting a deficiency here, strengthening a skill there. The children were asked to draw from nature instead of from a plan. The children from the second group were particularly educated to try to see something new, something unexpected in their models from nature. Realizing that this group was not naturally creative, the experimenters tried to inspire them to creativity by telling them fairy tales and asking them to draw some episode from the fairy tale.

The third group were asked to draw every line just as they saw it in nature, to draw a plan of it first, and to correct the plan as often as necessary to achieve a good result. All during the year the experimenters worked to improve the children's observation. In all their activities they were asked to observe how things looked, and how they differed from other things.

After eight months of work the differences between the three groups gradually were "liquidated." The second and third groups had both improved in their performance, and now all of the pictures were individual. Not one picture looked just like another, even in the second group. The experimenters had "taught" creativity to the children, and they attributed their success to the fact that the children had learned to draw from nature, which never presents quite the same picture twice.

Perhaps the difficulties of encouraging creativity have had something to do with it, but the 1969 *Program* has one revolutionary change in it. Now art classes for three-year-olds are divided according to ability, a practice which Soviet educators had disapproved of in the past.

The Soviets are not interested in art just for its aesthetic values, though that is an important part of it too. Art lessons have another valuable attribute: they furnish preliminary training for writing. The Soviets hope their citizens will have artistic taste. They *insist* that they know how to write.

Writing is considered to be even more difficult to learn than reading, as it requires even more abstract thought as well as more physical skills.

The physical skills have been taught to the child gradually, starting with correct posture while seated, the way to hold a pencil, and orientation of eye movements. Even before he is six, the Soviet child has had exercises to strengthen the small muscles of his hands. He has practiced catching a ball thrown at waist height to develop the arm movements he will need when writing in a seated position. He has gained finger dexterity by rolling forms in clay, cutting out paper figures and constructing houses out of blocks, paper and cardboard.

His ability to analyze a picture visually will help him to distinguish individual letters when he learns to read and write.

In addition to looking at pictures he has visual-dictation exercises in which he looks at tables showing combinations of lines and geometric forms, and then reproduces them in his notebook from memory. Sometimes the teacher indicates the pattern orally and the child must reproduce it on paper, whether it is a square, a triangle, a circle or some other form.

When he enters the school-preparation group at six he begins a course in writing. In September there are exercises to develop his eyes, his hands, and the small muscles of his fingers. He is also given a small blue notebook with about fifteen pages of paper covered with horizontal and vertical lines making small squares.

For his first lesson he outlines three squares. In the first square he draws six lines from top to bottom. The second square has six horizontal lines, and the third square has lines slanting downward from left to right. These are the basic strokes used in beginning writing.

In the second lesson the child combines an oblong box with vertical lines in it with two round balls containing slanting lines. These lines are made in three colors—green, red and blue. The third exercise consists of three balls with spiral lines. The spiral is begun in the middle of a circle and drawn from the center to the right, around to the left, around to the right, and so on, until the entire circle is filled.

In October the child draws lines from top to bottom, and from left to right, then incorporates these into patterns. The figures must be placed correctly in the notebooks and must combine lines of various sizes and slants.

By January, the child is beginning to make marks that resemble Russian letters, and is being taught to analyze his work on his own. He is asked to be particularly careful about rounding the nonstraight lines. The teacher demonstrates this rounding on the blackboard and the children describe large movements in the air with their pencils, so they can feel the correct movement. As they make these movements in the air they count, "One, two, three," so they are sure they are performing the motions in the correct order. To make the letter *R* (which looks like the English *P*) the teacher explains that to the straight line, which they know so well how to make, they must add a "helping" line and connect the two. The letters must be written between the lines on the graph-paper pages of the *tetrad*.

By the end of the year the children can write seventeen letters. The 1965 *Program* required only eleven letters by the end of the year.

·X·

Speech and Thought

IN STUDIES OF the interrelation of speech and thought, the name of Lev Semyonovich Vygotsky is an outstanding one, not only in the Soviet Union but in the world as well. Vygotsky's *Thought and Language,* although suppressed in 1936, two years after it was first published, appeared again in 1956; and today it and the books of Vygotsky's followers Luriya and Leontev are among the landmarks on speech and thought.

Vygotsky's book was an answer to *The Language and Thought of the Child,* by the Swiss psychologist Jean Piaget. Piaget, dividing the young child's speech into egocentric and social speech, concluded that speech was almost completely egocentric until the age of seven, when the egocentric speech died out and was replaced by social speech.

According to Piaget, before the age of six the young child's speech consists of an egocentric monologue in which words are repeated simply for the pleasure of talking. Even talk involving another person is more of a dual monologue than an exchange of speech, since the point of view of the other person is not considered. The child talks only about himself and does not even make sure that he is being heard. The socialized speech of the young child, Piaget said, is made up of adapted information, criticism of the work or behavior of others, commands, requests, and threats, and questions and answers.

Vygotsky, although acknowledging the value of Piaget's research in child perception, argued first of all with Piaget's assumption that egocentric speech does not fulfill a realistic function in the child's behavior. In experiments organized in the same way as were those of Piaget, Vygotsky showed that egocentric speech played a very important role in the child's activity. In Vygotsky's experiments a series of frustrations and unexpected difficulties were added to the child's task. When the child was getting ready to draw he would suddenly find he had no paper, or lacked a pencil of the proper color. Before starting the exercise, he had first to face a problem.

The child, in an effort to solve his problem, began to talk to himself: "Where's the pencil? I need a blue pencil. Never mind, I'll draw with a red one and wet it with water; it will become dark and look like blue."

In the same experiment, without difficulties, Vygotsky found little egocentric speech. This result was compatible with Piaget's theory that one becomes conscious of performing a usually automatic action when a difficulty is encountered, and that speech was an expression of that consciousness, but Vygotsky and Piaget drew different conclusions from the experiment.

To Vygotsky, egocentric speech marked a turning point in the child's activity. In addition to being a means of relieving tension, egocentric speech directed the activity and became an instrument of thought in an effort to solve a problem.

In another experiment of Vygotsky's, a five-and-a-half-year-old child was drawing a picture of a streetcar, when his pencil broke. He tried to continue his drawing with the broken pencil, but no line appeared on the wheel he was drawing on the paper.

"It's broken," he said, putting the pencil aside and getting some water colors with which to finish the drawing of the streetcar. With the water colors he painted a picture of a *broken* streetcar after an accident, his own words about the broken pencil giving him a whole new starting point.

An older child, faced with a problem like the broken pencil, may regard the situation silently, but when asked what he thought during this silent period, will say that his thoughts were much the same as those of the younger child. Instead of dying out, egocentric speech becomes inner speech. Egocentric speech is the link in the transition from vocal to inner speech.

Unlike Piaget, Vygotsky believed that the child's earliest speech is social communication.

Some of today's Soviet investigators believe that the newborn baby soon realizes that sounds can have meaning. At first he cries when he is hungry, wet or otherwise uncomfortable, but he soon finds that his cries bring an adult running to see what he wants and he realizes that "o-o-o-o-o" can be used purposely as a means of communication.

A. M. Leushina, of the Herzen Pedagogical Institute, says that the child's first speech is not a monologue but a dialogue. The "o-o-o-o-o" is a clear, concise expression of his wants, explicitly directed at another person. His cries are heard not only by his parents but by the child himself, and an association between the sensations of sound and the nerve centers of speech is set up. This association will have an important bearing on the way the child imitates speech sounds around him the rest of his life.

The newborn baby does not know how to talk. He is born into a world of sounds which he does not differentiate. He simply jumps when he hears a particularly loud sound, but at first he does not distinguish words from the other sounds around him. By the time he is two or three weeks old he is orienting to sound by turning his eyes in the direction of the sound, and when he is seven months old he is beginning to connect the sound of the voice of his mother with his bottle of milk or with the experience of being picked up.

The baby's own first sounds are indistinct. At the age of four or five months his sounds change character. Now they sound like recognizable syllables—"*ma, pa, ga, fu*," or, as another Soviet educator translated the words, "*beh, geh* and *yeh*." This educator, after talking to six-and-a-half-month-old Sasha for two hours one day, concluded that babies practice certain sounds on certain days. If this happens to be a "*beh*" day, the baby will respond to almost everything with a "*beh*." Since Sasha responded with thirty-three "*beh*'s," fourteen "*yeh*'s," and twelve "*geh*'s," the educator concluded that "*beh*" was *dezhurstvo* that day.

By the time the child is three months old the nurse in the *yasli* is trying to teach him to say *"ah."* She attracts the baby's attention by putting her mouth close to him and saying *"ah"* very distinctly. As the baby watches her he says something resembling *"ah,"* but when the nurse hides her mouth and says "ah" the baby cannot respond. He needs the reinforcement of his sense of sight for successful imitation.

At seven months the child sits where he can see the lips of his nurse as she says, "Kolenka [the baby's name], *ba-ba-ba.*" She repeats this several times until the baby tries to imitate her lips and make a similar sound. At other times, when the baby is on his stomach the nurse will say, "Kolenka, *polzi, polzi* [crawl, crawl]," as she puts a toy just out of his reach. If the child does not move, the nurse puts the palm of her hand against his feet and gives him a little shove. Then when he reaches the toy, he is allowed to play with it. When the child has learned the word for "crawl," the toy is put on the rail of his crib and when he reaches for it, he is helped to stand up, given the toy, and praised with the statement, "Kolenka stood up."

By the time the child is six or seven months old he can understand enough words to perform simple responses such as waving goodbye or clapping hand to *"Ladushki, ladushki."* Dr. Zaporozhets says it is the adult's tone that the child understands at this stage, rather than the words; and he shows that if the parents substitute *"Kapitan, kapitan"* for *"Ladushki, ladushki"* the child responds in the same way! However the word *bottle* makes him salivate just the way Pavlov's dog did when the bell rang. The word *bottle* is the beginning of a complicated second signal system which will be reinforced by more signals later.

In the final stage of babyhood, the period from ten to thirteen months, the baby can repeat *"da"* when mother or nurse say *"da";* and when she says *"da-da"* he also says *"da-da."* He can also say *"ma-ma"*—which is the same thing in Russian that it is in English.

In the *yasli* he has been carried around the room in the arms of his nurse since he was five or six months old, and shown mechanical toys which make noises such as a cow which says "*Moo-moo.*"

"Olenka, where is the cow, *moo-moo?*" The nurse asks, always using the child's name, the word "cow" and the sound the cow makes. As the cow says "*moo-moo*" the child turns his head toward the sound and the nurse says, "There is the cow, *moo-moo,*" and lets the child feel the toy cow. This exercise is repeated, sometimes with variations such as hiding the cow under a piece of cloth, then taking it off suddenly and saying, "Here is the cow, *moo-moo*, Olenka."

The "Magic Bag" is used to bring out other objects which are named and learned. A toy dog says "*av-av,*" while a goose says "*ga-ga-ga.*" By the time a child is a year old he should be able to answer correctly the question, "What does the dog (or cow or goose) say?" If the question "What is this?" or "What does the dog say?" is met with silence it usually means that the child has not had enough speech training and has not used speech as a means of social intercourse.

The value of such communication was demonstrated in an experiment in a *detsky dom* ("children's home" for orphans) when one group of very young babies was engaged in frequent conversation with an adult and compared with a control group which was left alone.

In the experimental group, an adult talked to the babies for seven minutes every other day, beginning with a minute and a half of soft conversation. Then the adult stroked the child's head and chest, and moved his arms and legs gently, while talking to him and smiling at him. In the last stage, the adult moved away from the baby a little, but responded to any reaction of the child with more smiles and conversation.

After the eighth seven-minute period of play and conversation the children were also given two minutes' play with a simple toy, and the movements of their hands, eyes and mouths and emotional responses such as smiles and laughter were noted.

Although it was found that the optimum benefit from these short conversations came when the child was from three to five months old, the experimental group showed decided differences from the control group even when a few months older. The experimental child was much more vocal, his movements were more developed, and he seemed happier. Even his physical development seemed improved by the happy emotional climate of the experiments. These differences were apparent after only thirty of the seven-minute sessions.

The emotional factor in speech preparation is extremely important. The more an adult talks to a child the faster he learns to talk. Group talking is not as effective as individual conversation.

Even before he can say the word, the trained child can recognize a *red* ball, a *red* pyramid or a *red* umbrella after he has been taught the word *red*. The use of the word seems to organize his thoughts. When he can talk, the word *red* gives him a sense of power. He will say, "This is a little red and a little not red," showing that he is ready to learn a new color.

By the time he is a year old, the child has come a long way both in physical growth and in speech. Learning to walk has opened up his world to new sights and sounds. His hands have developed so that he can manipulate various objects with some success. He is developing a sense of humor and can even play tricks on his mother such as hiding from her. He mimics words and even tone of voice.

Words also help him to orient himself in space as he begins to walk. He tests the words *near* and *far, left* and *right, up* and *down* with his own hands and feet, but his ideas of space are still so fragmentary that he thinks the moon is as close as the street light. He knows his way to his favorite toy or his mother's side, and in a few months he will be able to find his own apartment door when he and his mother return from a walk.

At a year and a half the Soviet child should know thirty or forty words, which he uses to express his wishes in social relations with adults. By two he knows two or three hundred words, and by the end of his second year he is using sentences of four and five words. The speech of the child is a means of acquaintance with his surroundings, and the speech of the teacher is a means of education for the child. The 1969 *Program,* stressing orientation to the environment, suggests that the teacher strengthen the child's new familiarity with words, first with the words of the objects themselves and then with attributes of the object—a pretty doll, a remarkable dog. The child is asked to repeat the words after the teacher to strengthen the nerve connections to the brain.

The more often the child can respond successfully, the more satisfied he becomes. Education becomes a rewarding emotional experience, and this pride in his own success is expressed in words—"I can," "I want to." Often the exaltation of self-expression takes the form of asserting his own independence against the adult. The command "Don't touch the watch" can be an irresistible temptation for the child to do just that. Little by little the child forms a fund of knowledge about himself in relation to others.

Adults say *"Nado* [You must]" or *"Nelzya* [You must not],"* and the child learns to respond, depending on how firm the adult has been in his admonitions and how consistent he has been in insisting on them. If the *"nado"* has been consistent, a new situation can be accepted placidly by the child with a *"nado."* Some moral and aesthetic meanings of words are also absorbed. *"Molodets* [good boy],"* *"khorosho* [good]"* and *"plokho* [bad]"* give the child some moral feeling of himself just as "pretty" and "amusing" give him some aesthetic values.

The child must know himself as an individual, separate from the people and things around him. By the end of his first year he should be getting some sense of himself as an individual. As he puts balls into boxes, fills his pail with sand and pours water through his fingers, the child is absorbing a feeling of self along with these physical sensations and abilities.

Sasha, at one year and four months, wanted to climb the stairs, but each time he lifted his leg in the manner to which he was accustomed, the leg just fell back in the old position instead of rising to the top of the next step. Finally he turned on his side and crawling like a crab, managed to get to the top of the stairs, where his mother discovered him, a little frightened by the height but exceedingly proud of his exploit.

"I did it myself," he says, and the word *myself* becomes an important one in his vocabulary from then on. When he did not want to take some medicine his father said, "Sasha, you are a man. You can take the medicine yourself. Do it yourself." The word "*sam* [(one-, my-, your-) self]" was a strengthening word— a signal of an independent self—and Sasha took the medicine himself.

The child's name has great meaning in the development of self-awareness. By the time he is a year old he should be responding to the sound of his name, but he still does not connect his name with what he will later call "I." The word *I* is the first step toward the knowledge of the self as a subject, as a personality. With a secure knowledge of himself, as *I,* he can relate to the other *I*'s around him in the collective and through these reactions and his relationships with others fulfill his potential as an individual member of the collective. He should not lose his individuality in the collective, but rather strengthen it as he sees himself in relation to others in his world. This orientation in time and space is important to developng an integrated personality.

Soviet games like "Terem-Teremok, Who Lives in the Tower?" and "Postman" help him to know his name and address and, incidentally, the names and addresses of some of his friends. "Postman" also asks the child to describe the package he receives in the mail, telling what it is used for and all about it.

The orientation of self in time is complicated, but again the relationship becomes clearer with the use of words. "Yesterday," "tomorrow," "evening," "morning," and other expressions of time are hard to assimilate. The child learns that it is dark at "night" and thinks he can tell "night" by this attribute, then along comes a dark winter morning in Moscow and suddenly the darkness that belongs to "night" also is called "morning."

Through all these complications and contradictions the pre-school child is gradually led along the path of development to the formation of ideas which are real abstractions. The development of ideas begins with the development of observation and memory. Soviet kindergarten children are asked to observe in detail what they see and then describe it in words or pictures or both. Sometimes they are asked to look at a picture and describe it. In describing a horse in a picture one child was amused to see how the horse's tail "jutted out" from his body, then she noticed that his four legs also "jutted out" as she said. Words concretize reality.

Memory and observation also depend on experience. One child taken to the circus enjoyed the unfamiliar experience, but when asked what she saw at the circus she had trouble remembering and finally answered, "There was a lamp there." Out of the unfamiliar sights she had picked one simple, well-known object, a minor object in the wealth of circus sights, but the child's "focus" was narrow because of her past experience.

Words become important in expressing more complex relationships. The words *because* and *in order to* answer questions, and questions are signals for specific orienting reactions of the thinking processes. Soviet educators feel that even two-year-old children can achieve primitive analysis and synthesis of thought.

The first stage of the thinking process is to formulate the problem into a question. Before you can solve a problem you must put it into the right category. What kind of information do you need to solve the problem? How has the problem been solved in the past? The two-year-old will start out with wasteful trial and error in his problem solving, but the Soviet educators hope to teach him a method of approach which will help him in solving all new problems, and they want to teach him the principles of abstract thought even in the kindergarten.

Verbalization is very important to analysis. The child who knows specific words can solve a problem better than one who doesn't know the words. In one experiment two groups of children were asked to match the pairs of nine butterflies of various patterns in three colors—red, blue and white. One butterfly in each color was striped, one spotted, and one patterned. Both groups of children were unfamiliar with the words *striped, spotted,* and *patterned,* but the meaning of these words was pointed out to one group, who were also shown the pictures of the striped, patterned or spotted butterflies.

The other group was not told these words, just asked to match the pairs. The children who had been told about the striping, spotting and patterning not only had more right answers than the other group, but were able to tell why they got the right answer: "These two have the same striping." In the other group the few children who happened to get the right answer could only explain it by saying, "I just knew."

Knowing various qualities by name can also save time. The child who has connected the taste with the word *bitter* will not have to test a lemon for himself, though the chances are that he will test it anyhow. Children taught the words *sparrow* and *swallow* to represent certain birds, easily coordinated the words with the general class of *birds*.

The Soviets believe that speech development is usually delayed with twins. Finding a set of identical twins in a kindergarten, Soviet psychologists studied them closely. The twins, Yura and Lesha, were the last children in a family with five other children ranging in age from nine to twenty-two. Both the mother and her brother had been late talkers, beginning to speak well only when they were eight years old.

At two years of age Yura and Lesha had not spoken at all, and at two and a half they could say only "ma-ma" and "pa-pa." At four they were using only short, undifferentiated phrases. Their mother could not persuade them to name a single object. In their play together they used very few words and these were just syllables of regular words, unintelligible to others. They did not seem to understand the speech of the children around them and did not seem interested in intercourse with the other children. They spent their time playing with each other instead.

Yura and Lesha did not seem to be mentally deficient. They were good, lively, energetic children, deft and rhythmic in their movements. They could feed themselves easily and knew how to dress themselves and gladly took on their duties in the kindergarten. Their play together was very primitive in form, and they never took part in complicated subject games.

They took no part in the play of other children, though if they heard another child cry they would listen anxiously to the cry until they were convinced that the cryer was a stranger to them. Then they would say in relief, "Lesya *nyet* [Not Lesha]" and *"Lyulya nyet* [Not Yura]" and go back to playing contentedly with each other. If they were separated, they tried to find each other again and cried until they succeeded.

Yura, as the weaker of the two, was selected for special speech practice. At first he responded to every one of the experimenter's efforts with complete silence, but after three months' work he responded with simple replies. Lesha did not receive special treatment during this period, and Yura's progress was noticeably greater than Lesha's.

The speech work with Yura consisted of dialogues between teacher and child, analysis of pictures through speech, and story telling. At the end of three months' training, Yura showed a noticeable difference from Lesha. Although Lesha had been the stronger and more active of the two until the beginning of the experiment, now Yura began, more and more often, to take the leading role in the games of the twins, which involved intellectual activities. In games involving running and motor activity, Lesha, being stronger, still maintained this leadership.

When the twins were given a picture of a mother, a child and a cat to describe, Yura would say, using baby talk, "The girl is crying. The cat is lying. Mama sits at the table." Lesha's words were: "Cat. Girl. Mama. Bed." Lesha disregarded verbs altogether.

In the primitive speech the twins had used with each other they could not separate the word from the activity it described. Even such intellectual operations as elementary classification were beyond the capacity of either twin at the beginning of the experiment. When the twins were separated and put in groups of normal five-year-old children they began to imitate the speech of the children around them.

Yura, with his special speech training, reached the conversational level of the other children sooner than Lesha, but the Soviet psychologists concluded that association with children more adept at speech was a sufficient stimulus to make the twins start talking normally.

Even the normal child, when he first comes to kindergarten, may have his ears so attuned to individual remarks made to him by his mother and the other members of his family that he actually tunes out all other speech. He may not hear the remarks addressed by the teacher to the class in general. To solve this problem, one teacher in Omsk uses two puppets, Petrushka and Rita, to address the class.

Petrushka and Rita invited the children to stand together in a circle and listen to a song, then walk around together, doing things the puppets told them to do, clapping their hands, running to a certain place or sitting down. The children, fascinated with the puppets, listened attentively for the signals and gradually became accustomed to a human voice which did not belong to someone in their own family.

Sometimes the listening process does not occur at home. One Soviet mother complained to her three-and-a-half-year-old son's kindergarten teacher:

"Misha won't answer when I call him. I can call him twenty times and he doesn't pay any attention."

"I think I can help you," the teacher said, and she outlined a plan.

The next day, the mother, following the teacher's advice, said casually to Misha, "I've been reading an interesting article about cosmonauts. Would you like to be a cosmonaut?"

"Of course," Misha said. "Everybody wants to be a cosmonaut."

The mother looked doubtful. "I don't know, though. It says here that cosmonauts have to have awfully good hearing."

"I have good hearing," Misha said.

"Really?" The mother was dubious. "Well, we might try an experiment. You busy yourself with your work, and I will go on with mine. Then, without notice, I'll call you and see if you can hear."

After that Misha was so attentive that he came running at the mother's first call and the problem was solved to everyone's satisfaction.

The child learns speech by listening to it and by using it himself. His mother is told to strengthen speech connections by discussing articles of clothing while the child is dressing, articles of food while he is eating. Idle, unrelated chatter may confuse the child.

Teachers too are cautioned to avoid stereotypes of speech. When children hear the same phrases over and over these become irritating noises rather than differentiated words. Children who are repeatedly told to sit "on the chair" think that "on the chair" is the word for chair. There is also specific work on such words as *on, under, behind,* and other words which narrow meanings. Comparison leads to the words *more* and *less,* both abstract words, and it teaches the child to analyze a new thing from his experience and to observe small differences in the new and the old.

If the children live in a republic with its own language, they learn Russian, and often a foreign language like English, German, or French, in addition to their own language. We watched some six-year-olds in the school-preparation group in a Leningrad kindergarten begin their English lesson, with the teacher saying, "Good morning, good morning to you. Children look at me. At me, look."

Then she explained to the children how her tongue "walked" around her mouth as she said, "Thank you. Three, th, th, th, that." The children, placing their tongues carefully in the correct position, imitated the sounds the teacher made, then said after her, "D, d, d, daddy, ding-dong, ding-dong. T, t, t, tick-tock, tick-tock says the clock."

The children did a short set of exercises to English words and then closed their eyes in a simulated nap, until the teacher said, "Wake up. You are not sleeping now, but Brother Joe is sleeping. Are you sleeping? Lazy Mary is sleeping. Let's sing the song for Lazy Mary. 'Lazy Mary will you get up?' " The children sang the Lazy Mary song together and then played other games which involved a knowledge of the English language, such as passing a cup around among them and saying, "I have a cup" or "I do not have a cup," depending on which was correct.

The children learn to count, with the help of their fingers: "One, two, three, look at me. I have two eyes, two cheeks, two ears, two hands, and ten fingers, one two, three, four, five, six, seven, eight, nine, ten. Dance little fingers. Dance little man, ring man, tall man, point man . . ."

The English lesson is given twice a week for twenty-five or thirty minutes at a time. It ends with a song, sung first in English and then in Russian.

So the children will not enter school with speech defects, remedial speech lessons are given individually to school-preparation children who need special attention. We watched one such lesson in a small room where the child and teacher were seated at a table. There was a paper bird hanging on a string over the table. When the teacher suggests that the child make the bird fly, the child blows the bird to a flying position. The child is asked to make various sounds as she watches her lip and tongue movements in a mirror. She is asked to exercise her tongue, to make it pointed, to spread it out, to show how a dog laps up water with his tongue. She learns the different positions and sounds for various letters—*s-s-s, z-z-z*, and some of the difficult Russian sounds. Throughout the lesson she is constantly praised and encouraged, to increase her confidence.

Distinctions in the meanings of words are particularly stressed in the year before school. Distinctions in grammar are taught also. Since the Russian language has three genders and six cases, with both singular and plural, and since every noun has a different ending according to case, gender, or number, there can be thirty-six different endings for the child to remember just for nouns. With verbs, there are the usual present, past and future tenses, but in addition there are imperfective and perfective forms. Adjectives agree with nouns in declension and have their own long or short endings. It is a rich language, but not an easy one.

The child learns grammar by continued practice in speaking. In the first year of school there is a noticeable difference between the child who has had training in kindergarten and the child who has not attended kindergarten; but now in the big

This preschooler is working on a speech defect. In the preschool institutions, much emphasis is placed on correct speech.

cities approximately eighty percent of the children have gone to kindergarten. A lower percentage of village children have attended kindergarten.

In an experiment involving children who had attended kindergarten and those who had not, both were asked to tell a story from their "life experience" as the Russians say. This particular life experience was the care and feeding of some rabbits in the nature corner of the school. The teacher asked who would like to tell about the rabbits.

Sasha, who had not been to kindergarten, volunteered: "We have in school a living corner. We have rabbits living in it. We bring them beets, cabbage, dried crusts."

Kolya, who had been to kindergarten, was asked to discuss the same subject and he said: "Rabbits are small, fluffy animals, resembling hares, with long ears and light-blue eyes. When I first saw them there were five—and I like them very much. They ran and roamed under the cupboard. I brought them carrots and cleaned them. They have white teeth. They began to gnaw and the rabbits made a face as though they were smiling. And when the white rabbit ate a beet, its mustache became red. In the spring the rabbits shed."

In addition to using many more—and more varied—words Kolya had a plan to his story, and also showed a real human feeling for his rabbits. He related to the rabbits much more than did Sasha. Of the stories told by kindergarten children, not one failed to give an outward description of the rabbits, the number of the rabbits, and their own relation to the rabbits. One kindergarten child, when telling his story, had his audience enthralled when he told how the rabbit he had picked to feed died. Most of the kindergarten children told of some concrete fact which occurred while feeding the rabbits. Their grammar and pronunciation were better than the nonkindergarten child, too, showing that their powers of observation extended not only to the rabbits but to grammatical structure as well.

It is in the social act of play that most children learn proper speech. A game called "What Did the Bear Find?" is used to teach orderliness as well as meaning. The teacher explains that the bear finds, and takes, all the toys that are not in their proper places. As she picks up the toys the children name them and tell where they belong.

Sensory perception is used in such games as "Taste It, What Is It?" "What Noise Does a Street Make?" and "Find the Colored Ribbon." In "Find the Color" the children sit in a circle and chant a poem, asking another child to find an object of a certain color. When the child finds it the other children chant, "*Da, da, ugadal* [Yes, yes, you guessed it]."

In "Uncle Comes from Polyanka" the teacher gives each child a colored bead, then she recites a poem about the uncle who carried colored beads with him. On the teacher's desk is a box, and when the teacher says, "Red bead—in the box," the child with the red bead must put it in the box, and so on, through the colors.

Most of the word games strengthen observation. A favorite is "What Has Changed?" in which the children are shown one picture followed by another, similar picture in which some objects have been changed. In "Find This Tree" the children are given a leaf and asked to match it with some tree on their daily walks, thus sharpening their observation and learning the names of the trees.

Phonetics are taught by a series of games stressing the sounds of various letters. "Wind in the fields" goes *"f-f-f-f"*; "airplane" goes *"r-r-r-r"*; and "train" goes *"sh-sh-sh."* The phonetic games, useful for normal children, are indispensable for children who stutter or have other speech defects. Stuttering children are asked to give the sound a whistle makes, the howl of a wolf, the cry of a baby, the hiss of a goose, the hum of bees, the drone of a mosquito, the roar of the wind and the sounds that dogs, cats, and other animals make. In his concentration and excitement at producing the requested sound, the stutterer forgets his handicap. Other phonetic games are played by deaf children to aid in teaching speech.

Habits of correct breathing, so important to speech, begin with simple exercises wherein the child breathes quietly through the nose and expels the breath through the mouth, saying *"f-f-f-f."* In other exercises the child is asked to smell a flower, while saying slowly that it smells good. A few educators disapprove of action games associated with speech, believing that the child's concentration is too divided by action and speech at the same time. Others think that action strengthens the word.

Role playing demands a larger vocabulary, because it is usually done in groups and the child's vocabulary must pass the test of being understood by others. The child whose parents have anticipated his wishes so much that he has not had to express himself in words now finds difficulty with communication.

Soviet psychologists feel that correct speech is very important to the psychophysical well-being of the child. Since speech is a primary means of communication, disorders of speech prevent social exchanges and lead to a sense of inadequacy and may even affect the physical actions of the child, as well as the intellectual development.

For older preschool children there are special kindergartens and sanatoria for correcting speech disorders. The children normally stay in these sanatoria for from three to six months. As soon as the children arrive they are given a thorough physical examination—the blood is tested, condition of the liver investigated, and particular attention is given to the speech organs, the lungs and the character of the child's breathing. The central nervous system is checked to see if some trauma of the brain may be affecting the speech, and the child's hearing is particularly investigated.

The first two or three days the child spends most of his time in bed, in what the Soviets call a "regime of silence," which gives him the maximum amount of rest in preparation for his treatment.

During the period of silence, the child may play quiet table games like Lotto or Dominoes, or listen to stories told or read by the teacher or therapist. The therapist, after telling the child something about a picture Lotto card, may then quietly ask the child to point to some object, without saying the name aloud. This strengthens words the child already knows, or teaches him new ones without the strain of having to say them aloud for the teacher.

Part of the therapy is the negation of negative emotions and the child must be made to feel that his fears of speaking are groundless, as he is taught faith in his own strength and abilities. The therapist tries to make him want to work for himself by strengthening his part in the collective.

As the child's speech improves, his social relations also improve and his anxious thoughts about his inadequacy fade. Even before the Soviets, the Russians attached great psychic significance to the child's native language. Ushinsky felt that the native language embodied all the things that made one nation different from another and that through the language the child became acquainted with the world of things, of people, their feelings, thoughts and interrelations. Through speech the child can learn to express his thoughts exactly.

After the quiet period in which he built up his confidence, the child in the speech sanatorium practices telling short stories about wild animals from stories he has been told. Such stories as the "Brave Hedgehog," or the Russian native tales "Teremok" and "Kolobok" are retold by the child, and when he can tell these stories in simple form, he advances to questions and answers and more difficult exercises. He is taught to listen—at first to sounds other than speech, like the rustle of paper, the sound of a spoon tapped on a plate, the sound of a ball bouncing on the floor. He is asked to close his eyes and guess what is making a certain sound. The therapist imitates sounds animals make, or hums a song, and the children guess who or what it is. Next the therapist reads aloud, and the child listens to the sound of her voice and tries to pronounce words she has read.

The children do tongue exercises and lip movements, and they practice breathing, rhythm and intonation as they repeat words and phrases. Games like "Echo" are used with two groups, one group saying *"a-a-a-a"* and the other echoing, *"a-a-a-a."* There are competitions to see who can pronounce the most syllables in one breath. The children learn which letters are formed with the lips, which are sounded through the nose, which escape through the "fence" of the teeth. They practice phonetics and learn the rudiments of grammar. So that they will be ready to write later on, they practice developing the small muscles of the hands and fingers.

The teacher shows the children subject cards ("Wolf," "Little Bears Bathing," and other pictures), and the child, with the help of the therapist, tells about the story the picture represents. Finally the child is ready for the last phase of sanatorium learning—the stage of spontaneous speech. Now the children are asked to improvise in games like "Post Office," "Store," "Times of the Year" and "Professions."

The aim during all the stages of instruction has been the building of self-control. The children are taught to analyze their own speech and that of their comrades. They learn to watch for too-slow or too-rapid speech. They learn poems and plays to present to the parents when they come to the sanatorium on Parent's Day.

Parents represent a problem in many instances, so both children and parents are carefully prepared before they meet in the sanatorium. The children are cautioned not to forget the rules they have learned while talking to their parents, and the parents are informed of the regime of the school, told of books they should read, shown how they can follow their child's progress and given other information, such as the time and place of

parents' committee meetings, the office hours of speech specialists and when seminars on speech problems will be held. When
the child is well enough to leave the sanatorium, the parents,
hopefully, will be able to continue the child's speech training at
home.

The speech training in *yasli* and *detsky sad* is probably the
most important single contribution the preschool institutions
make to the school child. From the first *"o-o-o-o"* the child is
taught to communicate with others; and teachers who can
talk to the children are praised, and teachers who require silent
obedience are censored.

By the time the child is ready for school at the age of seven
he must be able to tell a simple story, pronouncing his words
clearly, and including descriptive passages which add to the
interest of the story. Tests disclosed that children who were
asked questions about a picture they were shown were able
to describe it better than children who had not been asked the
questions. The most important question was "Why?" In an
experiment with the fairy tale of the bear who had a peacock
tail, the experimental group was asked, "What are the animals
doing? . . ." "In what position are the animals?" . . . "Why
are they in that position?" . . . "Where will these actions lead?"
The control group was simply shown the picture and asked to
describe it.

The control group said, "The bear walked," while the experimental group said, "The bear walked merrily, and said,
'Ah, how beautiful I am with my peacock tail. All the other
bears will die of envy!' The bear's eyes were shining and his
ears pricked up and his nose was in the air."

Besides having a more emotional reaction to the picture, the
experimental group noticed specific movements of the animals
and seemed to enjoy the story more. Eighty-five percent of the
experimental group noticed specific movements of the animals,
seeing psychological causes for these physical expressions, while
only twenty percent of the control group characterized the movements from an emotional standpoint.

The child also learns how to care for his voice. Three-year-olds who are inclined to speak too loudly or too softly are taught to regulate their voices through games that teach correct breathing and exercises that correct speech tempo and rhythm. The children are taught to save their voices—"Don't sing outside in cold weather. Try not to shriek. It may injure your voice."

There are games that teach clear pronunciation of Russian sounds such as *geese*. (The Russian word for *geese* sounds like our word *goosey*.) In the game, the children gather at "home base" until the teacher calls, *"Goosey, goosey, goosey."* The children answer, *"Ga, ga, ga."*

"Do you want to eat?" the teacher asks, and the children say, *"Da, da, da* [Yes, yes, yes]."

"Well, go nibble some grass," the teacher says and the children stray away from home base. When they are some distance away, the teacher says suddenly, "White geese, go home. A gray wolf is coming over the hill." The children run quickly back to home base, the wolf after them.

The children are taught appreciation of their native language by listening to the sounds of cultured Russian speech, both when the teacher speaks and when she reads them stories and poems by great Russian authors.

It is not until the school-preparation age (six) that the children begin to regard speech as a classroom subject. Now speech becomes something to be studied more seriously, as the foundation of school subjects, particularly reading and writing and arithmetic.

·XI·

Learning to Read and Count

SOVIET STUDIES HAVE found considerable difference in the ability of children to learn without tiring. The two-and-a-half-year-old child tires after nine to thirteen minutes, while the three-year-old can work for nineteen minutes. The child tires more quickly when he does not understand the problem or when he does not have the ability to solve it.

In one experiment, two-year-old Andreyusha was asked to select one particular card of two shown to him and gladly gave the experimenter the correct card when asked for the "blue one" or the "red one"; but when he was asked to select a particular card from fourteen cards he quickly became distracted. The following day he came to the experiment gladly, sat on his chair and looked attentively at the two rows of fourteen cards, then he stood up, waved to the experimenter and left the room. The next day he came to the experiment but did not look at the cards. When the experimenter suggested that he do the exercise he got up and left the room. The fourth day he refused to come to the experiment at all.

To avoid such situations the Soviet educators go about teaching very gradually and carefully. The child's first lesson in abstract thought does not seem to be a lesson at all, and it comes when the child is learning to talk. His first word is an abstraction for some thing. He learned that *cup* meant the object which contained his milk, and later that *cups* was also a group and contained not only his cup but also Mother's teacup. He learns to analyze; he begins to put things into groups, to find the common quality, to notice what distinguishes one object from another. This is the beginning not only of logical speech, but also of logical thought.

The *yasli* and *detsky sad* try to create a definite rhythm of life for the child and one of the main components of this rhythm is order. Order is also the basis for arithmetic. The shelves for toys are arranged in an orderly fashion—dolls on one shelf, toy machines on another. Balls are in a large basket-ball-net type of basket, building materials in a special corner. Everything has its place according to its group. In the group are some objects which are exactly alike. These pairs are *equal.* Some other pairs are *unequal.* The child learns *large* and *small* and *more* and *less.*

By the time he is four he himself feels the need to learn numbers to describe *more* and *less.* The four-year-old learns to count to five, but he also is taught to look for the result of counting and to distinguish the result from the process. In counting, the teacher asks one child to stand in front of the class, as the other children count "one"; then another child is asked to stand by the first child, as they count "two"; and so on, up to five. Now there are *five* children and this is a *result.* The *process* of counting is over. As the children sit down one by one, the counting is done in reverse, five, four, three. . .

Several senses are used in counting. The children close their eyes and listen to a number of claps. They close their eyes and feel how many mushrooms there are in a basket. They watch to see how often the teacher makes a certain movement. They compare one group of three dolls with one group of two dolls and learn that three is more than two and that numbers are a way of describing a certain attribute of things. By the time they are five they can count to ten and have mastered the conception of the relationships of numbers.

Objects are arranged in rows, like the children in front of the class, and numbers are applied to them. Gradually the children see that the numbers form a definite system which tells them something specific. Now five children line up touching each other, and five children stand behind them with a foot of space between each child. The second line is longer than the first, but does it contain more children?

Five balls are counted out and put beside five dolls. How are the two groups alike? How are they different? In all the problems the effort is to present the problem in a slightly different way from the way the child has previously learned, so that he must think and apply the principles he has learned to the new task. The Soviets do not want the child to rely on mechanical memory.

The children learn that arithmetic is different from reading, that arithmetic asks for some kind of number as a solution to the problem and that the question asked about the problem is usually a clue to the solution of the problem. Now they learn that instead of counting, one, two, three, in a problem asking how many three and two are, they can work in units. In subtraction the children learn to subtract the smaller number from the larger.

In the school-preparation group, each child has his abacus on the table beside him. In stores and businesses the Soviets also use the abacus, and even when they have calculating machines, they usually check the figures on the abacus. For the math class each child has his own compartmented bag with cardboard numbers in the pockets. The teacher has a large cloth bag hung by the blackboard. In one class we watched there were also counters in the shape of numbers, plates, glasses and spoons lying on each table beside the abacus.

"Take out three and five," said the teacher. "Five is more than three, and both are more than one. Take off one, and how many do you have left?"

A girl in red is very quick and counts out the answer at once. Her seat mate in a blue dress with red polka-dot panties is upset. She takes out her counters uncertainly. The girl in red reaches over to help her. Finally the teacher comes over and explains in a soft voice.

The numbers are put away and a sheet of white paper is folded in half three times and carefully torn across the folded lines. Each child now has eight small pieces of paper. "Do you have more than you had to start with?" "Show me one eighth of the paper." "Show me three eighths of the paper." "Now

listen very carefully to a very hard question. What do we have
if we have eight eighths? A whole page!"

Next the same principle is illustrated with a bowl of uncooked
rice. "If we want to know how much rice is in the bowl, what
do we do? It would take a long time to count each grain
wouldn't it? We have two glasses on each table. Suppose we
take the rice a spoonful at a time from the bowl and put it in
the glasses, and every time we put a spoonful in we move a
yellow counter on our abacus, to add for us."

The children start putting rice into the glass, but all try to be
careful and finally everyone has the rice in the glasses, and each
abacus shows a different number of spoonfuls.

"How many spoonfuls of rice in your glass?" the teacher asks
a blond boy.

"Seven," the boy says.

"How do we speak correctly?" the teacher asks.

"I placed seven spoonfuls in my glass," the boy says, correcting himself.

They discuss the reasons for the differing number of spoonfuls in everyone's calculations, then the teacher takes two glasses
of rice and pours them in two piles on a table. "Which pile is
bigger? Both the same?" She spreads one pile out into a big
circle with the palm of her hand, "Now which pile has more
rice?" Two children come up to the desk and examine the piles
intently. One pile definitely looks bigger.

"It seems to me that this one is bigger," one boy says pointing
to the spread-out pile. "Just seems to be more," another child
says.

"We will put it back into the glasses and see," the teacher
says. She scoops it back into the glasses and by some miracle,
despite the scooping and spilling, the glasses manage to have
the same amounts of rice in them.

For the children who have not gone to kindergarten, these
lessons in arithmetic are shown on television, and we saw the
lesson on the two piles of rice repeated in several programs in
different Soviet republics.

With the speeded-up program in the primary school it is

even more important that the kindergarten child have a foundation in math. The 1969 *Program* puts more stress on math learning than the 1965 *Program,* and this trend will probably continue. Now the first-grader must know the theory of arithmetic operations and how they are related. He must know that addition and subtraction are inverse operations, as are multiplication and division, and that multiplication is a special form of addition. He must understand mathematical forms and how to use them, that the sign $>$ means "is larger than," and the sign $<$ means "is less than." He must also know what is meant by "compare the expressions," "verify the equality," and "verify the inequalities."

Even in kindergarten the child is taught how to approach a problem, how to devise a plan for solving the problem, what questions to ask himself, and how to put these questions in the language of a numerical formula. The formula permits the child to grasp the whole problem at once, saves time for the pupil, and makes it easy for the teacher to check to see whether the pupil understood the problem. Each problem must contain something new, so that the child does not develop a stereotype.

The plan for solving a problem is concise:

1. Read the conditions of the problem attentively.
2. Imagine to yourself what the problem is about.
3. Draw a diagram to show the content of the problem.
4. Write down its conditions.
5. Read the problem again and think what you need to know to answer it.
6. Make up a plan for solving the problem
7. Perform the necessary operations to get the answer.
8. Verify the answer.

The Soviet educators believe that the child of five or six has a normal desire to learn to read and that if he were not taught to read he would learn to read by himself. "What is this letter?" he asks or "How do you write *V*?" He tries to read by letters, and when he goes to the first grade the teacher will have to retrain him, since in his letter-by-letter approach he will make many mistakes in trying to put words together without a systematic knowledge of the letters. Bad habits are hard to break; it is easier to teach a child who does not have to unlearn something before he can learn correctly.

It is even better if the child comes to first grade with a beginning knowledge of reading. The teaching of reading in kindergarten began as early as 1956 in some schools in the Baltic republics, and now is taught in many schools in the Russian Republic and some others. In most cases it is just beginning reading, but there will still be a difference between the children who have had this beginning instruction and those who have not.

Even before the Preschool Institute was created, the preschool section of the Institute of the Theory and History of Pedagogy of the Academy of Pedagogical Sciences was investigating methods of teaching preschool children to read and write. Experiments in the fifties started with developing word discrimination. The basic sounds of language were compared with the written letters. Thirty-two activities were prepared, mostly in the form of games, to prepare the eyes and hands of the children for reading and writing. The children, sitting at desks sat facing the teacher, on whose desk were some toys—an elephant, a goose and a duck.

The teacher, holding up one of the toys, said, "Children, we can say a sentence about every one of these toys. Listen while I say a sentence: 'The doll sits.' Now, see if you can make a sentence."

Other lessons followed, all designed to develop sight differentiation and the ability to articulate the elements of the whole word. The muscles of the hands were trained for writing movements and the children were shown where to start on a page, writing from left to right. The children's attention was trained so that they could accompany the teacher's word explanations with the proper actions.

Reading, writing and arithmetic are considered similar activities and in the beginning the foundation for all three is geared so that the instruction benefits all equally. For reading, the child in the school-preparation group will usually have at least two periods (of twenty to twenty-five minutes each) of reading activities every week, such periods being interspersed among other activities as in this rather representative schedule:

Monday:	Instruction in telling a simple story
	Counting
	Drawing
Tuesday:	Preparation for reading
	Physical Training
	Observation of nature and the life of people
Wednesday:	Preparation for writing
	Musical activity
	Appliqué work, modeling or construction
Thursday:	Preparation for reading
	Counting
	Instructions in storytelling
Friday:	Preparation for writing
	Musical activity
	Work in appliqué, modeling and construction
Saturday:*	Listening to the reading of stories of literary merit
	Drawing

The first activity, for the month of September, involves understanding the sentence as a means of communication. Thoughts are expressed in words, the teacher says, and when words are connected with each other, they form sentences. She holds up various toys, which the children name; then they repeat, after the teacher, that these names are also called *words*.

"Everything we see can be expressed by words," the teacher says. Then she drops a ball on the floor and asks the children to make up a sentence of two words showing what happens when she drops the ball.

* Even though most parents are now on a five-day work week, they do not all have the same day off, so most kindergartens are open at least half a day on Saturday.

"Ball falls," one child says. *The* is not used as a separate word in Russian, but is implied. The teacher throws the ball to Sasha and asks another child to make up a three-word sentence. "Sasha caught ball," he says correctly.

This is the Soviet child's first analysis of living speech. The game is repeated with other objects, as the teacher writes the words on the blackboard, with some lines beside them to represent the number of words:

Ball ———
Ball falls ——— ———
Nina throws ball ——— ——— ———

The second exercise also involves the composition of a sentence and the division of a sentence into words. The children use albums of colored pictures and try to match the pictures with words printed on other sheets. Sometimes there is just one object on a page—a rake, a hoe or a pair of pliers. Other pages may have a carrot, a turnip, and a flower on the same page. There are three printed words to a page, and the child must select the pictures that match the words.

Radina has an attractive book of colored posters; it is called *Repka* and is a favorite story as well as a musical game. The story tells of an old grandfather who lives in a hut by a pretty white birch tree. Grandfather, with grandmother's help, spades up a garden and plants a turnip, waters it when it is dry and cares for it tenderly until it gets so big he can't pull it out of the earth. Finally with help from his grandson they get the turnip out of the ground and eat it, and there is much excitement in the meantime.

Besides reading the story of *Repka* (*Turnip*) the children are reminded of other objects whose names they know. They try to name as many vegetables as they can, try to remember riddles about the vegetables and guess the riddles. Sentences without prepositions are analyzed. The teacher suggests certain sentences by the questions she asks. If *Repka* is used, the children are asked for details of the fairy tale, and they make up two- and three-word sentences about the people in the fairy tale.

The words are written on the blackboard, the number of words in a sentence being marked by green dashes. The sentences are then broken down into their parts again. The children observe that it takes two expirations of breath—that is, two sounds—to say some of the words; and the teacher tells them that each expiration is a part of a word and is called a *syllable*.

The third exercise for September is the division of the word into syllables. The teacher tells a story of a little girl who calls her friends. They do not hear her so she calls louder:

" '*Ma*-sha! *Sa*-sha! *Tan*-ya!' Why does she call them like that? Why doesn't she just say 'Masha, Sasha, Tanya'? That's right. They can hear better that way, because the word is clearer."

Then she asks the children to watch her mouth as she says the word *papa*. She shows how she opens her mouth twice. The children put two blue dashes on the blackboard. They put their hands under their chins as they say "*pa-pa*" and see for themselves how many times their mouths open. In all childhood learning Soviet educators try to bring in as many of the senses as possible.

Next, the teacher says the first part of a word, and the children try to guess the second or third syllable—*kosh-ka* (cat), *so-ba-ka* (dog). From a pile of toys, the children divide the name of each toy into its syllables.

The last exercise in September acquaints children with one-syllable words. On the children's desks as they come into the exercise, are pictures turned picture side down. The children go over what they now know about words and syllables, then they turn their picture cards over. The teacher wants to know who had a picture of a two-syllable word, who has a three-syllable word?

In October the children take up letters and sounds. There are thirty-two symbols in the Russian alphabet, but there are forty-two basic sounds. In October, November and December, the kindergarten children learn eleven of these sounds—four vowel sounds (*a, u, y* and *o*) and seven consonants (*m, sh, r, s, l, n* and *p*).

Since *a* is the first letter in the Russian alphabet, the children start with that. They learn to pronounce the letter correctly. Then they think up words which begin with the letter *a*. They pronounce *a* with other letters and separately, noticing how freely they can pronounce it; their breath comes out without any interference. They listen for the letter *a* in words—at the beginning, in the middle or at the end of words.

The teacher shows them a model of an *a*, then they model *a*'s themselves out of clay. They color cutout cardboard *a*'s with red pencils. On the blackboard hangs a big picture of a stork with the letters *a-i-s-t* under it. They divide the word *aist* into *a* and *ist*. Two syllables. "A" is also a word itself, ("while," "and," or "but" in Russian). They draw pictures of all the objects they can think of which begin with the letter *a*. They look at the proper page of the book *Alphabet in Pictures*. At the next lesson, they review what they have learned about *a*.

By the end of November they are beginning to learn a little grammar as well. If someone named Masha is called to the blackboard, the sentence "They sent Masha to the blackboard" will read "They sent Mashy to the blackboard, because the *a* changes to *y* in the accusative case. Any grown American who has studied Russian will be surprised if kindergarten children find Russian grammar easy, and grown Russians must feel some sympathy too, because they were very tolerant of mistakes in my grammar. I hated to speak in front of the children, fearing my grammar would not be up to kindergarten standards.

The lessons with sounds continue, each lesson beginning with a review of previous lessons and sounds. In December they come to the sound *r*, which the Soviet find is a difficult sound for children to pronounce correctly.

"What does the dog say when he growls at a cat?" the teacher asks, and fortunately Russian dogs growl in the same way American dogs do, even though they don't bark the same way.

"R-r-r-r," growls the dog, say the children. The teacher shows the children where the tongue is when they say *r*, and they practice it, feeling the position of the tongue in their mouths. They learn a poem where the blackbird says, *"Kar, kar, kar,"* so they may say *r* rapidly and clearly.

By the end of January they know enough letters to start

reading. The teacher brings out picture cards 5 by 8 inches, with slots along the bottom edge. The cards show large pictures of a watermelon, a boat, a balloon, a rose, a mushroom, and other familiar objects. One by one the cards are put up on the blackboard, and one child is invited to go up to the board to put the letters that belong with each picture in the slots at the bottom.

At the desks, each child has his own bag of letters in pockets, and he takes out the proper letters, putting the vowels on the left and the consonants on the right, after they have spelled the word.

Usually there is a little conversation about the picture before the exercise begins, or the teacher may tell a story involving the pictured object. After the object has the identifying letters placed in its pockets, the word is read out loud, syllable by syllable—and as a whole, for analysis of its sounds. The sounds of one word are compared with a similar one of different meaning —ma-ma is compared with Ma-sha. The children repeat the sounds in unison and individually, and change the letters in the little pockets on their own desks, substituting the *sh* of *Masha* for the second *m* of *ma-ma*.

By the end of the year the children have learned how to construct a short sentence, telling how many words it contains, and naming the order of the words. They can divide words into syllables, understanding that syllables are pronounced in one breath and always have one vowel. They can read a short sentence and explain its meaning.

One reading teacher in a kindergarten we visited was particularly proud of her class. "We will show our guests how we get ready for school," she said to her class, in Russian. "Our guests are from America. Tanya will you write the sentence so we can read it?"

Tanya goes to the big bag of cutout letters hanging on the blackboard, and the teacher asks, "What is the first word?"

"*Nashi,*" everyone says, as Tanya takes the letters out of the letter bag and places them in slots on a large board next to the bag. Each child has a similar slatelike board on which to put his smaller cutout letters.

Spelling lesson—arranging letters to make words. When reciting, posture is important. Soviet children do not slouch.

Word by word, the children spell out, "Our guests are from America." A big red dot is put at the end of the sentence.

As the teacher reads the sentence aloud she sees that a spelling rule is involved. *"Nashi* [Our]," she reads; *"n, a, sh"* (н, а, ш, in Russian characters). "What is the rule?"

"After *sh* [ш], there is always *i* [that is, и], not *y* [that is, ы]," Tanya says, and all the children recite the rule after her.

Now all the words are put back in the bag except the word for "guests." "Suppose we just had one guest, how would we write it? If the guest is a woman? A man?" A girl with tarlatan bows on the ends of two long braids, her hands stiff at her sides, answers and shows the symbol for the Russian "soft sign." All the children are very serious.

When all the letters are put away the children stretch their arms before taking up an *azbuka* (alphabet). Each child has a small pointer the size of a nail file and points to each letter, as they read aloud. "We know how to read and write," they read slowly. Then they recite the alphabet and read a short poem by Samuel Marshak.

"This is a remarkable book," the teacher says. "You can read about plants, about machines. You can see the whole U.S.S.R., or read about your favorite fairy tale. The *key* to this book is right here—in the alphabet."

It is playtime again, and the girls go to the doll corner and the boys to the model Kremlin they are building as they take an "active" rest period. Then the teacher says, "Ready for the next activity? Tuck your shirt tails in and go quietly to your tables."

This time the reading game is in the form of acrostics. One child spells a word on the board with letters from the bag. If it is *D-O-M* (house), the next child is asked to change one letter and make a new word. The *O* is removed and *Y* put in to spell *D-Y-M* (smoke).

When the lesson is over, the children often go to the book corner, with a little library table and chairs beside some bookcases filled with children's books. There the children can "read" for themselves, spelling out the words they have learned in class.

·XII·

Books for Everyone

THE SOVIET PEOPLE have a passion for books. We sometimes saw excited crowds gather on a Moscow street, as if there had been an accident or a riot, only to find that a street bookstall was selling a new edition. Books are inexpensive and, though printed in up to 750,000 copies, sell out almost at once. Pedagogical, scientific and mathematical books sell almost as fast as books of fiction and poetry. The large bookstores everywhere are jammed with people.

Detskaya Literatura (Children's Literature), a publishing house, publishes two thirds of the children's books, with more than six hundred titles a year and a total printing of 125,000,-000 copies. The readers range in age from three to seventeen, and the publisher's catalogue specifies the appropriate age level for each book. The books sell from about 4 kopeks for paperbacks to 90 kopeks (there are about 110 kopeks to the dollar) for the more expensive hard-cover stories.

We came home one day to our Kiev hotel room and found the maid sitting on the sofa reading one of the children's books I had bought. She looked up at us pleasantly; "*Khoroshaya kniga* [Good book]," she said, without taking her cotton-stockinged feet off our coffee table.

The book she was reading was one of the most popular of children's books, *Moidodyr*, by Kornei Chukovskii. A great deal of the charm of the story, as it is in Pushkin's poems, is due to the beautiful rhythm of the Russian language. The sound of the words themselves express the brisk race of bedclothes, samovar, toys, clothes and other inanimate objects away from a dirty little boy. The story finally ends happily but only after the dirty boy cleans up.

Chukovskii's life spans the whole period of Soviet power, from the Revolution to the present day. Despite his constant popularity, his works have not been without criticism. No less a person than Krupskaya herself, criticized his fairy tales.

Krupskaya, who believed that most fairy tales were "saturated with petty-bourgeois psychology," particularly disliked Chukovskii's poem "The Magic Tree," about a man who had a great many children who needed shoes, but very little money with which to buy shoes. In the poem the man finds a magic tree which grows shoes and stockings:

> *Come, all you children,*
> *Come and see!*
> *Your heels are bare?*
> *Your snowshoes rot*
> *You need new shoes?*
> *This is the spot!*
> *Your boots are ripe,*
> *Your shoes are done,*
> *Stop loafing now,*
> *Come, pluck them, run!*

Krupskaya wrote an indignant review of this poem, which she felt was in definite opposition to the Communist ideal. She thought people would believe that Communist children were still divided into rich and poor as in the past and that only a miracle could provide them with new shoes.

"Children do not need this nonsense," she wrote. "I find all these very silly fairy tales disturbing and irritating. I think that "The Magic Tree" should not be reprinted."

"Children do need fairy tales," Chukovskii said, "and if they are deprived of them in storybooks they will improvise their own tales." Chukovskii was disgusted with people who "view each children's book as a tool which must immediately produce tangible, useful results. They fear fantasy and imagination though they themselves, as revolutionaries, were dreamers out of touch with the reality that prevailed around them."

When Chukovskii's fairy tale *Krokodil* (*Crocodile*) was criticized and prohibited, the prohibition was protested by such authors as Alexei Tolstoy, Konstantin Fedin, Nikolai Morozov, and others. The protest resulted in permission to publish a small number of copies, though a few months later the prohibition was renewed.

In 1929 Chukovskii started another controversy when he read *Adventures of Münchhausen* to some sick children in a Crimean sanatorium. The sanatorium director interrupted Chukovskii's reading and said that neither Chukovskii nor *Münchhausen* was welcome in her sanitarium. The argument was taken up by the Moscow education specialist E. Stanchenskaya, who supported publication of a pamphlet by E. Yanouskaga, "Fairy Tale as a Factor of Class Education," which stated that fairy tales were harmful to Soviet children.

Chukovskii's tale *Mukha-tsokotukha* was severely criticized too. The Commission of GUS (State Learned Council) thought this tale expressed admiration for the kulaks (rich peasants who were liquidated by Stalin), just as *Krokodil* was criticized for being about Kornilov's mutiny, although it was written a year before the mutiny. Chukovskii's tales were accused of fostering superstition and fear, and giving an unrealistic view of animal life. Parents and teachers were warned not to read these books to children and were urged to protest their publication and use in schools.

Chukovskii did not defect to the West nor did he go to a concentration camp. He continued to write. He said, "Each time the Children's Literature or the Young Guard publishes a children's edition of *Hiawatha, Just-so Stories, Poems of Pushkin* or *Münchhausen,* these suppressors of childhood scream, 'the Revolution is in danger,' and they run to defend the revolution from Pushkin and his poems!"

In 1934, at the first national meeting of Soviet writers, the famous Maxim Gorky came to the defense of fairy tales, and books like *Hiawatha, The Little Humpbacked Horse,* and some of the Greek myths began to appear in the bookstores again, though they were often followed by indignant letters to the editor.

By 1956, fairy tales were again in official Soviet favor, and Soviet journals even spoke of how fairy tales enriched and humanized the Soviet child, showing the ideals of justice, goodness and freedom. However, Chukovskii was still deploring the practice of Soviet educators who selected and changed the fairy tales to suit Soviet aims. The Commission for Children's Literature continued to disagree with Chukovskii's point of view, though Soviet parents still bought Chukovskii's books and Soviet children continued to enjoy them.

In 1960, preparing a new edition of Chukovskii's book for parents, *From Two to Five,* the editor said he did not think the chapter on the fairy tale dispute was necessary any longer, but a reader showed that interest in the subject was very much alive when he wrote a letter objecting to Chukovskii's marrying a gnat to a fly.

Today most letters to the editor favor fairy tales. Young mothers and grandmothers want to know, "At what age should I give my children Pushkin? And when should they read Mayakovsky?"

Other letters complain that they can't find Chukovskii's *Mukha-tsokotukha* in the bookstores. *"Tsokotukha?"* a saleswoman in Riga says. "We had it here two or three days ago. Sold out."

A father in Novosibirsk, unable to buy the book at a store, asked all his friends to look for it, so he could give it to his son. He was overjoyed to receive the book by mail from one friend, but his joy did not last. The book was written in Georgian. Now, he wrote the editor, "Just as soon as I can get a Georgian-Russian dictionary I'm going to translate the story for my Andreyushka."

A reader in Baku wrote that of the thousand customers in any Baku book store in the middle of the day, every second one of them wanted *Mukha-tsokotukha.* A reader in Leningrad said that he was going to put an advertisement in the paper:

"Wanted: a nurse who loves children and knows the fairy tales of Chukovskii."

Chukovskii himself died in Russia in October 1969 at the age of eighty-seven, leaving an estate of over a million rubles. His works survived his critics, and before he died he was honored with the Order of Lenin and three orders of the Red Banner of Labor.

Chukovskii and others like Pushkin, Gogol, and even Lenin himself, were influenced by the rich heritage of Russian folklore which may have developed, as Marx suggested, as a compensatory cultural form which often springs up in backward nations. In Tsarist Russia, folk tales were often a sly method of criticizing the government. The peasant developed tough powers of resistance. Seeming compliance with the Tsarist regime was undercut by folk tales, which became a defiant weapon of class conflict.

The old folklore contained wedding ceremonials, funeral laments and laments for departing soldiers, as well as the *byliny* (epics), proverbs, riddles and tales which today's children love. The tales, generally divided into magical, legendary, romantic, and foolish-devil tales, were first collected in 1838, but one of the most important collections was *Russian Folk Tales,* by A. N. Afanasyev, which appeared from 1855 to 1866. These tales were divided into animal epos, myths, and tales of everyday life. By the twentieth anniversary of the Revolution, the Soviets thought highly enough of Russian folklore to publish *Creative Art of the Peoples of the U.S.S.R.,* a work which had been instigated by Gorky and prepared by the *Pravda* staff.

Elijah of Murom is the favorite hero of the *byliny* and is known to every preschool child. Although Elijah is a son of the peasantry he is not afraid to speak the truth to princes. For thirty years Elijah (or Ilya, as he is also called) sat motionless, unable to move his arms or legs as his brothers worked in the fields.

One day three *straniki* (the eighth-grade Russian reader identifies these as "people who go about on foot, usually devout people") passed by and asked Ilya to bring them some water. Ilya said that he could not, since he was without arms or legs.

"Get up, Ilya," the *straniki* said. "Don't deceive us."

Some variations of the story say that the *straniki* gave Ilya three draughts of a miraculous drink which gave him remarkable strength, but in any event, Ilya got up and went about his amazing exploits.

Ilya's first great feat was the slaying of the Nightingale Robber, a huge bird with supernaturally powerful whistle, whose nest stretched over seven oaks. Ilya set out to find the Nightingale Robber, but, like Hercules, he found many obstacles in his way. At Chernigov, Ilya defeated a large Tartar army single-handedly and then found the Nightingale Robber. Ilya struck the Nightingale Robber on his white breast and then tied him to his bridle, dragging him back to the Nightingale Robber's palace. One of the Nightingale Robber's daughters picks up a flagstone weighing one hundred pounds and is about to throw it down from a castle window on Ilya when the Nightingale calls out that the stone will kill him too, so the daughter puts it down.

At the court in Kiev, Ilya's story about the great Nightingale Robber was not believed. The court asked him to have the Nightingale Robber demonstrate his powerful whistle as proof of Ilya's story. Ilya, realizing the power of the whistle, asked the Nightingale Robber to whistle at half strength, but instead the Nightingale Robber whistles full strength and all the houses shake and the window panes drop out of the windows. In punishment, Ilya cut off the Nightingale Robber's head. Despite his victory over the Nightingale Robber, Ilya was still not popular with Vladimir's court and was given a low place at the table below all the princes, boyars and merchants.

Ilya set out on other exploits and was always victorious. Finally, an old man, he came upon a stone with an inscription on it pointing out three paths. One path lead to wealth, one to marriage, and a third to death. Ilya felt that he did not need wealth, and he was too old for marriage. If he took a young wife she would just be a burden to him, and an old wife would only lie on the stove * and be useless to him; so Ilya chose the road to death. On the road were forty thousand robbers, but Ilya killed them all and thus avoided death. Then he took the road to marriage, where he met a beautiful Amazon with a deceptive bed, which sank down to a depth of forty *sazhens* (about 225 feet). Ilya threw her on the bed first and she sank down and was buried; so he escaped marriage.

Then he took the last road, the one to wealth, but when he found caves full of gold and silver, he gave it all to the Church and the orphans, so he escaped wealth too. His death came quite suddenly later, when he was fighting. He and his horse turned to stone and he became a monument of Russian strength.

Another favorite *bogatyr* is Dobrynin Nikitich, who married the Amazon after striking her with his club three times without hurting her. At the third blow she remarked that she felt some gnats were biting her. She then seized Dobrynin by the hair and put him in her pocket and carried him around for three hours before deciding she liked him well enough to marry him.

The Amazon remained faithful to him for some time, but as Dobrynin was away on business for some years, she finally married his friend, Alyosha Popovich. Dobrynin's horse told him of his wife's remarriage and he returned to a reunion with her. He was not angry—because, as he said, with all women, the hair is long but the memory is short.

The ballads of the *bogatyri* are characterized by constant epithets and repetition. Children are delighted with the traditional formulas the narrator uses—formulas for saddling a horse, a formula for the knight's arrival at court, and so on.

Marx said that even though folklore was part of the childhood of society, it was not devoid of charm, and Engels and Lenin thought folk tales could be used to serve social purposes. After reading from the collection of his friend V. D. Bonch-Bruyevich, Lenin said that on the foundation of the folk tales one could

* In Russian peasant homes, the space on top of the kitchen fireplace-and-oven was the main sleeping area for as many as six or seven persons.

write an excellent study of the "hopes and expectations of the people."

Today the favorite Russian author of fables is still Ivan Andreyevich Krylov (1769–1844), who satirized the corruption and stupidity of the ruling class of his day. Besides translating the fables of La Fontaine, Krylov wrote nine volumes of fables himself.

Soviet children also read the fables of Andersen and the Brothers Grimm in Russian translations. They are particularly lucky, too, that the greatest Russian authors have also written stories especially for children. Tolstoy in particular, wrote many famous children's stories, as did Ushinsky, Turgenev and Gorky. Children also have poems of Pushkin and Mayakovsky. No children in the world have better literature for their first books.

My favorite children's story by Tolstoy is the story of the lion and the dog, which starts out with the surprising statement that in London people who want to see wild animals (presumably in a zoo) either pay money for admittance or bring dogs and cats to be eaten by the wild animals.

One man wanting to see the animals threw into the lion's cage a dog that he had picked up on the street. The dog tucked her tail between her legs and lay down in a corner of the lion's cage. The lion came over to sniff at her, and the dog turned over on her back and waved a paw at the lion, who did not hurt her. When the keeper brought the lion his meat the lion left a piece for the dog to eat. At night the lion and the dog slept together.

One day a lad came by, recognized his dog and asked the keeper to give her back to him, but when the keeper tried to get the dog out of the cage the lion roared so, he left them alone. For a year the lion and the dog lived together happily, until one day the dog became sick and died. The lion stopped eating, just paced back and forth in the cage, roaring. He would not even let the keeper take the dead body of the dog out of the cage. The keeper thought he could divert the lion by putting another dog in the cage, but the lion simply tore the new dog to pieces and embraced the dead dog in his paws. For five days he lay there with the dead dog, and on the sixth day the lion died.

Of the more cheerful modern fairy-style characters probably the most famous is Chukovskii's Dr. Aibolit who has many adventures with wild animals, including a crocodile. Dr. Aibolit begins in a particular Russian way with the expression *"Zhil-byl"* which is the Russian equivalent of "Once upon a time," though it means "There lived."

Two other writers particularly popular with the kindergarten set are Samuel Marshak and Agniya Barto. Marshak's books are good-sized paperback books with large illustrations and rhymed verses about all sorts of things from wild animals to the rescue of a child from a burning building by an unknown hero.

Agniya Barto's book *The Contrary Boy* tells of the boy who always does everything backward, while her *Mashenka* tells of a little girl's day. Other Barto stories tell of life in summer camp and the fields, and of holidays, like New Year's Day, when Ded Moroz brings presents to the children.

Soviet children read Nikolai Versilin's books about plants, Lev Uspensky's books about words, Yakov Perelman's books about mathematics, physics and astronomy. They enjoy the stories of Boris Zhitkov, Arkadi Gaider, Mikhail Prishvan and Lev Kassil as well as translations of *Gulliver's Travels, Uncle Tom's Cabin, Winnie the Pooh* and *Don Quixote*. Older children like books by Jack London and Mark Twain.

The most widely distributed children's book is *How the Steel Was Tempered,* by Nikolai Ostrovsky, the story of a young man who, though wounded, blinded and paralyzed (like Ostrovsky himself), never stopped working for his country. This novel for older children has been published in fifty-two languages with a total of more than nine million copies since 1945, when it was first published. The head of the literature section of the Institute of Artistic Education told us that the book was now required reading in school, and he added wisely that the fact that it is required makes it less popular now. His Institute does not have charge of preschool reading, but he told us fourth-to-sixth-grade children wanted to read about heroes, while the eighth-to-tenth-grade children were more interested in ideals.

Soviet Life points out that very young readers do not always understand the moral of the stories. In the popular story *The Dragonfly and the Ant,* the ant, who worked hard all summer storing food for the winter while the dragonfly sang and danced, refuses to help the destitute dragonfly in winter.

"You sang all the time, didn't you?" the ant says. "Now go ahead and dance!" A five-year-old retelling the story said, "The dragonfly was a merry thing, she sang and danced all the time. But the ant was an angry thing, he would not let her in his house."

While fairy tales are now accepted and children are encouraged to read them, horror tales about witches, fire-breathing dragons, and monsters are considered harmful, and parents are advised not to allow them.

One Soviet writer tells what can happen when children are told horror stories. Lyuda's parents wanted her to grow up to be a brave and fearless girl. Lyuda was quite fearless about animals like cows and dogs, and she was not afraid of the dark until she heard a story of an eight-headed, fire-breathing dragon who stole little children from their beds at night. That night Lyuda insisted that her mother stay with her when she went to bed, and after she finally fell asleep, she awoke, crying: "He'll eat me, he'll eat me, he'll carry me away!"

The author comments: "Needless to say, a reaction like this does not make a child any braver and is definitely injurious to his nervous system."

Little Nadya, "a smart and levelheaded child of eight," was seriously affected by tales of witches, so that when walking through a dark wood, she insisted on holding on to her adult companion's hand, who asked, "What's the matter? Surely you're not afraid?"

"I'm not afraid, but I always see little witches sitting on the branches, wanting to jump down on me," she answered.

"But you don't believe in witches, do you?"

"No, I don't," Nadya said firmly.

After a moment, she went on to explain, "When I was small I was told a lot of stories about witches. I don't believe in them now, but when it's dark and I'm all by myself I keep seeing them just the same."

Soviet children do not believe in Santa Claus either. They may, however, believe in Grandfather Frost, who performs the same services for Soviet children that Santa Claus does for American children. Grandfather Frost—or Ded Moroz, as he is called in Russian—has an assistant, the Snow Maiden (a sort of female snowman) who helps him to deliver presents. Ded Moroz and the Snow Maiden do not come on Christmas, because the Soviets don't believe in Christmas, but he comes at the New Year's celebration in January and leaves toys around the fir tree, which is decorated like our Christmas trees.

Whether or not Soviet children believe in Ded Moroz is not important to the Soviet state. It is important that they believe in Lenin and what he stood for. Nineteen seventy is the one hundredth anniversary of Lenin's birth, and the Lenin stories and pictures are intensified in all the kindergartens.

It would take a very unusual child to dislike Lenin from the stories, as they are warm, human and interesting, showing that writers can follow the party line and still write well. My favorite Lenin book is a collection of stories by L. Kon, telling about Lenin's childhood in Simbirsk (now called Ulyanovsk after Lenin's family name of Ulyanov). The book has pictures of Lenin's family's house, a fair-sized wooden building, with neat, clean rooms, and it shows Lenin taking exams for the Simbirsk Classical Gymnasium, playing with his friends, and sitting in a family group at home.

Kon's book, *O Volodye Ulyanove* (*About Volodya Ulyanov,* Ulyanov being Lenin's real last name and Volodya being the nickname for his first name, Vladimir) tells about Lenin's life at home with his family and the old nurse, who read fairy tales to the children and told them about how hard it was to live under the Tsar.

Lenin's sister, Olga, asked why the Tsar, if he wanted to,

couldn't arrange everything better, and Lenin said he didn't know. Perhaps they had better ask Sasha. (Sasha, Lenin's older brother, was executed later, for his part in an abortive attempt to murder Tsar Alexander III). When Lenin and Olga asked Sasha about the Tsar, Sasha simply shrugged his shoulders. Why should the Tsar tell the landowners to help the peasants, he said, "You know the Tsar is a landowner himself."

When Lenin went to the Gymnasium to take his examinations he saw a number of other boys there for examinations too. Among them were two boys Lenin nicknamed (to himself) "Blue Shirt" (because the boy wore a blue shirt) and "Prince" (because the boy looked like an illustration for the Prince in the fairy tale "Zolushka").

Blue Shirt had a hard time with his recitation, which was part of a test. The teacher hurried him along and harassed him at every word. Prince, who looked as though he were more accustomed to marble halls than to grubby schoolrooms, had chosen Pushkin's "Winter" for his recitation; but halfway through he stopped abruptly, obviously having forgotten the rest of the poem.

"Never mind, never mind. Don't be upset," the teacher said. "We can see that you know this poem and undoubtedly many others." Prince returned proudly to his seat.

When it was Lenin's turn to recite, he chose "Muzhichok—Nogotok," which he knew perfectly, as well as the questions of grammar that were part of the examination. Lenin was accepted. He liked the school very much. Among the pupils were some rich boys who couldn't even dress themselves. Lenin laughingly told the boys that his sister could dress herself when she was only two years old, but the boys continued to talk about how much money their fathers had, who had the best horses, who had the most servants.

One day one of the boys said, "Hey, Ulyanov, do you have servants?" knowing that Lenin did not have servants, but hoping to embarrass him.

"Oho!" Lenin said. "Yes, I have two servants, just for myself. They do everything that I want them to. They not only shine my shoes, they even wipe my nose and defend me against block-heads. You don't have such servants. Here they are!" And Lenin held up his two fists.

There were very few poor boys in the Gymnasium, but there was one whose father was too poor even to buy him a notebook. The rich boys told him that their fathers said that a Gymnasium was no place for such boys and Lenin answered that *his* father said that a Gymnasium must teach *all* children.

Krupskaya said the books about Lenin's childhood, although praising him for always getting fives in school, should not show him as a priggish child by any means. The books say that he loved merry, noisy games and could not be called a "quiet" child. Even the stories of him as a grownup emphasize his human qualities.

The story, "Play in the Snow" in *Krasnyi Mak* (*Red Poppy*) tells of Lenin working in his study during a snowstorm. All day the snow fell, until everything, including the black jackdaw sitting on the cornice outside Lenin's window, was white with snow.

At four in the afternoon, Lenin went in to his secretary: "Lydia Alexandrovna," he said, "I feel like doing something unimportant."

He went out onto the street and soon ran into some children having a snowball fight, which Lenin joined. When he got back to the office, rosy-cheeked and snow-splattered, his secretary commented on how rested he looked and asked him to remind her to take such a walk the next day. That night the lights in Lenin's study burned late, as he worked, even harder than usual.

Most of the books show Lenin with children—nephews, children of friends or even children he had never met before. They tell how Lenin spent New Year's Day with school children, how he picked mushrooms with them, and worked with them. The propaganda is never blatant.

V Smolnom (*At Smolney*), which was printed in an edition of 750,000 copies and sells for four kopeks, tells of an old peasant from Siberia who goes to Petrograd (Leningrad) to see Lenin. At Smolney he hears Lenin speak to the workers and peasants of the revolution. As he is leaving the building the old man is asked by a guard if he told Lenin about his life. "No," says the old man, "It was *Lenin* who told *me* about *my* life."

There are other stories about Lenin by Krupskaya, by his friend Bonch-Bruyevich and by other people who knew him. The stories (and pictures) show Lenin's love of nature, his affection for his cat, his dogs. They always relate to the child's own world with sympathy and humor.

In the kindergarten there is a book corner with bookshelves and chairs, where the children can go to look at books or read them if they are able, or they may select a book for the teacher to read to them. They are taught how to care for books, and on their walks they visit libraries and sometimes a book-repair shop, where they are told more about the care of books.

"You can tell a lot by looking at a book," a bookbinder told one kindergarten group. "You can tell what its owner was like."

He picked up a book of Russian fairy tales. "Now look at this book. Its owner loved books. See how clean the dust jacket is? The book was wrapped up in paper and put in a bookcase or on a shelf. Its owner was good. He not only read the book himself, but he gave it to his friends to read."

He picked up another book, a tattered, rumpled book, with pages torn from it. "Tell me who the owner of this book was?"

"*Strepka-rastrepka,*" the children said, as they shouted the Russian expression for a slovenly person.

Children have their own magazines too—*Murzilka,* and *Veselye Kartinki* (*Merry Pictures*), with cartoons, stories and verses. There are stories about animals, like "Willy, the Circus Elephant," stories of everyday life, and stories of Soviet heroism. Children also have their own moving pictures, like the movie about the circus lion who went to Africa on a holiday, but found so many little African children who had never seen a circus lion, that he spent his whole vacation performing.

For teachers there is a whole library of books, the Ushinsky Library in Moscow, with special departments for books about preschoolers. All of the people we met at the Preschool Institute had written authoritative books on their special subjects, and at times it seemed to us that there were almost as many people writing books as there were reading them.

·XIII·

The Teachers Taught

TEACHERS ENJOY a much higher status in the Soviet Union than they do in the United States. The Soviet teacher is respected as the propagator of Communist ideals and a person who plays an important role in forming the personality and character of the younger generation. She also bears great responsibilities. When a child fails an examination, the name of his teacher is sent to the Department of Education, which then checks on the teacher to see if her teaching was at fault.

The kindergarten teachers learn their jobs at a pedagogical *uchilishche* ("college"), which they enter at fifteen or sixteen years of age, after finishing the eight- or ten-year elementary school. If the student has finished the ten-year school she will take a two-year course in the pedagogical college, but if she has finished only the eight-year school, she will take a three-year course.

The teachers of the pedagogical colleges are in turn taught by teachers trained in pedagogical institutes. Admittance to the pedagogical institutes is by examination, and twelve or thirteen girls apply for every one who is accepted. In both the colleges and the institutes, girls from rural schools must meet slightly less strict requirements for admittance than girls from city schools, since rural education is slightly inferior, and the authorities are interested in encouraging rural graduates to go back to their villages to teach. There is a shortage of teachers in rural areas, most young people preferring city life, despite inducements of collective and state farms.

The pedagogical *institute* does not train teachers for work in kindergartens, but only for work as teachers in the pedagogical *colleges.* We visited the Hertzen Pedagogical Institute in Leningrad, which contained two *kafedry* ("chairs" or "faculties"), the preschool faculty and the *nachalnaya* ("beginning") school faculty.

The Hertzen Pedagogical Institute is a nice-looking building in the Leningrad style, with a statue of Ushinsky in front of it. We went up the stairs to the office of the director of the preschool faculty, A. M. Leushina, a very remarkable woman. We could hardly believe that Professor Leushina had started work in 1924. She had enormous vitality despite what must almost certainly be close to seventy years of age.

"Did you know Krupskaya?" I asked, and she smiled.

"I heard her speak twice," she said. "She was a remarkable woman."

Professor Leushina explained the work of the Institute, telling us that there were twelve pedagogical colleges in the Russian Republic and thirty in the other republics to train kindergarten teachers, and thirty pedagogical institutes with preschool faculties to train teachers for the pedagogical colleges, and also to prepare methodists and inspectors for preschool institutions. Most of the pedagogical institutes have day, evening and correspondence courses, with the daytime course taking four years to complete and the evening course five years usually.

The four-year course proceeds according to a regular plan, starting with the "methodology cycle," a general course in philosophy, history, history of the Party, economics and sociology.

The next cycle continues the general education with basic work in biology, anatomy, physiology, hygiene and pediatrics. Then there is a schedule in psychology, with emphasis on child psychology, and seminars on both foreign and Soviet psychology.

The last cycle is the pedagogical cycle. The history of pedagogy is studied, including Western, Russian and Soviet pedagogy. The methods of Froebel (the nineteenth-century German educational reformer who gave the world the word *kindergarten*) and Decroli, as well as the system of Montessori and methods of teaching specific subjects like physical training and art are also studied.

Lectures and discussions are held on such subjects as the social role of education, moral and mental education, and the development of the personality. The influences of the Octobrists, the Pioneers and the Komsomol on the child are also discussed.

In the first two courses on pedagogy the students listen to lectures and observe a teacher teaching in a pedagogical college. After the third course the students go to a kindergarten for practice. They must learn how to teach in a kindergarten, even though they will not do this after they graduate. The authorities feel that the teacher must know how to teach in a kindergarten herself, before she can teach others to teach in kindergarten.

There is also practice teaching in pedagogical colleges. The students listen to and read papers, and practice lecturing on various pedagogical subjects. The fourth course includes more practice and special courses for methodists and inspectors. When the student has finished the four-year course at the Institute, she must take a state exam on Communist ideology, psychology, pedagogy, and methods of the chosen field. There is an examination on the subject the student will teach as well.

Directors of kindergartens must attend a pedagogical college and two years of a higher school, and work for three years as teachers before they can become directors. Most graduates must work where they are sent for several years after graduation, though personal preferences are allowed where possible. Shortly before graduation, lists of vacant teaching jobs are sent to the various pedagogical colleges and institutes, and the students may ask for particular places on the list.

The Russian language, being very rich, has a number of words which we would translate as teacher, but in Russian they imply different grades of accomplishment. The kindergarten teacher is usually known as a *vospitatel,* which implies "up-bringing" or "training," as opposed to more formal education. Upbringing is the foundation of character on which education is built, so the *vospitatel,* even though she has not had the scholastic work of higher-school teachers, is a very important part of the system.

The teacher in the primary grades is called *uchitel* and the teacher in the higher grades is a *prepodavatel*. If the graduate of the Institute wishes to continue for a more advanced degree he may prepare a dissertation after a three-year minimum of advanced study, during which time he is known as an "aspirant." The pedagogical institutes at Perm and Kiev have courses for aspirants. The aspirant must pass exams on basic knowledge of psychology and sciences, a second exam on philosophy, and a third exam on a foreign language. Finally, he must defend his dissertation. If successful, he will receive the degree of Doctor of Pedagogical Science (if his work is in education). Postdoctoral work of two more years, if successful, leads to the title of professor.

We were duly impressed with *Professor* Anna Mikhailovna Leushina of the Hertzen Institute, though her manner was simple and modest in spite of her accomplishments. She gave me an unpublished mimeographed program for the 1969–70 school year of the Institute. This interesting document contained detailed plans for the work of the Institute, and as she had told us, the work was divided into four parts, the first part being concerned with general problems of pedagogy, among which were the goals and tasks of Communist education.

The Soviet people are particularly interested in discussing moral themes, and the classes in Communist theory have some lively sessions. Future teachers want to know the answers to all kinds of questions:

"Is Communism the ultimate goal of mankind or will there be an even better system?"

"Will there be physical labor under Communism if everything is automated?"

"How will women live and work under Communism?"

"How will the withering-away of the state take place?"

"What will be done with people who violate Communist rules?"

"How must one prepare oneself for Communism right now?"

The students also study contemporary bourgeois theories of ethics and the bourgeois theory of moral education. Methods of teaching respect for the motherland and the teachings of

Lenin are also studied, as well as atheistic education and the eradication of religious superstitions. Pedagogical tact is advised in handling parents who are believers. These parents must be shown how their religious beliefs can interfere with the happiness of their children, but the teacher is advised to do this tactfully.

Understanding the goals of education is one of the greatest problems for young teachers, according to one Institute professor, and understanding of subject matter is the next most important problem.

Both are stressed in the pedagogical colleges, such as Pedagogicheskogo Uchilishche No. 3, *imena* N. K. Krupskaya (Krupskaya Pedagogical College), which we visited in Moscow. Krupskaya College has both day and evening divisions, and seventy-five percent of the girls there are "on stipend"—which means that they are paid while attending college.

The girls studying to be kindergarten teachers study the theory of preschool education, methods of work with children, and anatomical, physiological and psychological peculiarities of children and how to handle them. They learn the elements of scientific atheism, how to acquaint children with nature, how to teach physical training and all the other subjects essential for a kindergarten teacher.

In the first year the student has a course of general studies, with 348 hours of math, 238 of physics, 231 of literature, 200 of history, 181 of chemistry, 160 of a foreign language, 89 of social science, 80 of biology, and 72 of economic geography, plus a tremendous amount of physical education.

The second year is devoted to anatomy, physiology and hygiene, and psychology, plus methods of teaching language, art, singing, physical education, and other subjects. The greatest number of hours is spent on the methodology of developing speech (272) with those of singing (252) and drawing (251) following. Pedagogical practice, including practice teaching in a kindergarten, occupies 422 hours.

The political education of the girls is considered particularly important in a period in which they are being subjected to capitalist propaganda and in a time when capitalistic theories are infiltrating the Soviet Union and endangering Communist ideology. The history of the Party and the history of the U.S.S.R. is studied in and out of class. Excursions are made to the Lenin Museum, the Museum of the Revolution, and the Marx-Engels Museum; and the girls attend lectures and watch films on such subjects as "The Beginning and Course of the First Russian Revolution," "The Movement for Communist Labor and Life in Our College," "Krupskaya and Work Education," "Themes of Revolution and Civil War in Creative Art," and "Literature about Lenin in the Educational Work of the Kindergarten."

Twice a month the girls attend lectures on atheistic themes such as "Soviet Laws about Religious Cults," "Individual Work with Believers," and "The Struggle against Superstition." Two bulletins are published by the college on atheistic themes—*Religion and Children* and *Militant Atheism.*

The girls are constantly reminded of Ushinsky's statement that the teacher can teach only as long as she herself is learning. When she stops learning, the teacher in her dies. The class leader is responsible for inspiring the girls to learn and to increase their general cultural level with concerts, visits to art museums, and reading. The class leader must know the girls' backgrounds, must help them with their personal problems, and must organize talks on how to strengthen the Soviet family, what the Soviet government has done for children, and when and how to teach children.

The college also publishes a *letopis,* or yearbook, about the life of the various college groups, meetings with interesting people, sports results, the history of each class, announcements of meetings and films, and some humorous stories.

There are the usual clubs for photography, dancing, art and drama, and a big chart in the entrance hall shows the girls how to dress, the most becoming way to wear their hair, and other beauty tips. Most of the girls are only eighteen when they graduate. They giggle and blush and run about like healthy, normal girls anywhere and delight in putting on entertainments —which reminded us very much of the entertainments we saw in the kindergartens.

The director of Krupskaya College invited us to watch an

"artistic concert" put on by the girls of several of the clubs. We went into a crowded auditorium with, at one end, a bare stage without curtains. Two girls in the front row gave us their seats as the concert began. A pretty, dark-haired girl gave a recitation about a rabbit and a turtle. Other girls danced and sang, singly and in groups. The girls in the audience leaned forward with the same rapt attention we had noticed in the kindergartens, and when the concert was over they helped each other on with coats and scarves just the way the kindergarten children did.

The making of successful teachers is the goal of the pedagogical colleges, but Soviet educators realize that teaching is an art as well as a trade. Pedagogical tact cannot always be taught. The experts praise the way one new teacher handled her first class:

"Devochka [a familiar expression for 'girl']," the children said to her, "did you come to play with us?"

"What is your name?" another child asked, using the familiar "thou" instead of the formal "you."

The girl was a little confused, not knowing how to correct the familiarity. Then she realized the children themselves had shown her how to deal with them.

"Yes, I came to play with you," she said, bending down to them. The director of the school smiled. The new teacher would be all right.

Pravda and *Uchitelskaya Gazeta* (*Teacher's Newspaper*) and *Doshkolnoye Vospitanie* all have articles on the better teachers and the "secret of their success." An article in *Doshkolnoye Vospitanie* tells of Vera Alexandrovna Milutina, whose kindergarten was like one big happy family in which the children were lively and playful, ate with good appetites, and slept well.

When she was asked what she did when the children would not listen, she said that there was no standard recipe, but she recalled an incident that happened to her on a walk with the children. Vova and Tolya ran off from the group and climbed a tree, but in getting down Vova fell and scratched himself. Vera

Alexandrovna gathered the children around her and asked them to "feast their eyes on a hero" and see how Vova had "decorated" himself.

Then she said that Vova was unsuccessful because climbing a tree was hard work. It was all right to climb trees, she said, but it should be done with the teacher's permission, because she was responsible for the children's lives.

Later that day the children were playing "frontier guard" and decided the patrol would climb a small tree. Everyone wanted to be the patrol, but the children excluded Tolya and Vova. "Today they have already climbed enough trees," the children said.

Vera Alexandrovna used community opinion and action to a large extent in managing her group. If a child could not accomplish a task alone he could ask help from a comrade. The children cleaned the bookshelves, painted boxes, changed the water in the aquarium and, after the game, even made some toys themselves.

One day Vera Alexandrovna noticed that someone had defaced the bookstand with a crayon. Lyuda, the child on duty that day, would not tell who had done it.

"We will not go for our walk today until we know who marked up the bookstand," Vera Alexandrovna said. All the children were silent. (Today depriving the children of their walk is not recommended.)

She asked the children to hold out their hands. All did, except the tree-climbing Vova, who put his hands in his pockets. The other children looked at Vova, who cried out suddenly, "It was I who covered it with drawings."

"It is good, Vova, that you confessed," the teacher said. "Now the children know that you are not a coward."

After setting things in order, Vera Alexandrovna took the children for their walk and on the way she told them about Vova. He had no father, his mother was sick, and though he himself behaved badly, he was kind and sympathetic. She asked the children to include him in their games and be friendly with him.

Teachers, like Vera Alexandrovna Milutina, who excel in their work are given the Krupskaya medal, a round medal with Krupskaya's picture on one side and a hammer and sickle on the reverse side, with the words "U.S.S.R. For service in teaching and Communist education."

Grading the child is one of the difficult problems the teacher has to resolve. Sometimes parents are as displeased with too high a grade as they would be with too low a grade. A teacher, writing of her experiences told of a child named Valya who was very smart but could not stand to be rebuked for anything.

One day the teacher noticed Valya, elbow on the table, with her head resting on her hand, carelessly writing in her notebook.

"Valya, sit up as you should. And what are you scrawling in your notebook? You know how to write beautifully," the teacher scolded.

Valya did not answer. She changed her position and bent over her notebook. The teacher noticed that Valya was offended by the sharp criticism and, to placate her, gave her a good grade on her work, even though it was not up to her usual standards. Valya smiled ironically, shrugged her shoulders and, closing her notebook, threw it aside.

The next day Valya's mother called the teacher. "Mariya Pavlovna," the mother said, explaining that she, herself, had taught school for fifteen years, "be careful about giving out grades. Overestimated grades only spoil the pupil. As a matter of fact, yesterday, noticing that my Valyusha was doing her homework carelessly, I said to her, 'Valya, you're not even trying.' And she said to me, 'Why should I try? It's all the same to Mariya Pavlovna. She'll give me a good grade anyhow!' Excuse me, Mariya Pavlovna, but listen to an old pedagogue. Never think you can placate a pupil with good grades. It only spoils the child, and you risk losing your authority over the children, because the children secretly joke about every incorrect mark."

The teacher accepted the criticism and the next day she gave Valya a "two" on her homework, and wrote below the two: "Think for yourself, why a '2'?" (Five is the top grade.)

A Soviet doctor once watched a group of three-year-olds in a kindergarten in Minsk. After washing their hands they sat quietly on their chairs, hands on their knees, without moving or talking, waiting silently while the nurse prepared dinner. Their teacher said proudly, "Look what a disciplined group I have. Nobody stirs."

The doctor noticed that the children were restraining themselves with great difficulty and were sitting quietly only out of fear of disturbing the strict demands of the teacher. Although some teachers restrain their children this way, it is not the goal of Soviet education, and some doctors think that such prolonged quiet sitting is harmful to the child.

Modern educators disapprove of the teacher's constantly admonishing the children—"Petrov, sit down! Pankov, put your hands on your knees." (Children when sitting in a chair must have both feet firmly planted on the floor, hands on their knees.)

Physical punishment is forbidden, and making the child sit in a corner is discouraged, though some parents and teachers still use this form of punishment. The teacher should not deprive the child of food, send him to bed, or deprive him of his walk as punishment. Thus, one of the few punishments left to the teacher is to make him sit in his chair quietly while he thinks over his misbehavior. When one inspector saw four children sitting in their chairs as punishment, she asked what they had done wrong.

"They don't know how to behave on a walk. They throw sand."

"Don't they like their toys?" the inspector asked.

"Toys? We don't take them on walks."

This teacher, the inspector thought, was more guilty than the children. If the children had been allowed to take their toys along, they would have been too occupied to throw sand.

Occasionally indifferent mothers cause trouble. "I asked Mama to cut my nails, but Mama said she didn't have time," a child says; and the next time the mother brings the child to school the teacher gives her a pair of scissors and a little talk. It would be easier for the teacher to cut the child's nails herself, but this would be relieving the parent of a responsibility and is not encouraged.

Vladik's mother was a yard keeper, who made very little money. Vladik was always poorly dressed at school, with worn shoes, and no buttons on his clothes. In winter he had no scarf or mittens or rubbers. He came to school with fingernails dirty, and with clothes and body unwashed. His mother found little time for him.

When the teachers spoke to Vladik's mother, she replied that she had no money. The teachers tried to show her how she could at least sew on the buttons and wash the child's shirt, but the mother took no interest. The teachers decided they would have to make the changes themselves, so they cut Vladik's nails, mended his shoes, sewed on his buttons and washed him every day. Soon Vladik came to the teachers of his own accord when he needed a button sewn on.

At the New Year's celebration one of the other mothers in the school gave Vladik some blue trousers. Another mother gave him some mittens. Vladik's mother was touched by the attention and the presents. She began to take more interest in Vladik's appearance, and before long Vladik appeared in a splendid velvet suit his mother had bought for him. Apparently her interest in Vladik had led to more initiative on her part and a better-paying job.

Parents are asked to help the child, but the child must also do his part. The Soviet state worries particularly about developing spoiled children, and parents are cautioned not to do too much for their children. Tolya's mother told how she handled Tolya when he forgot to clean his shoes before going to school.

"Mamushka," he said, "You clean my shoes, or I'll be late for school."

"Clean them yourself, and be late," Mama said. Tolya began to cry, but he cleaned his shoes. He cried and cleaned, cried and cleaned. When he was finished, he ran as fast as he could to school—and was happy to find he wasn't late after all.

Kindergarten directors are urged to persuade parents not to

leave children in preschool institutions more than five days a week, and children who do not see their parents during the week receive extra attention from the teachers to make up for lack of parental care.

Teachers try to persuade parents to set good examples for the children and to speak softly to each other. The child at school is asked, "How can we help Mama?" or "Who helps Mama at home?"

Parents whose children do not attend *yasli* or *detsky sad* are also invited to attend lectures given by the Academy of Pedagogical Sciences on such themes as "One must begin with the education of fathers," or "The training of children and their parents."

Understanding the child often teaches the parent when to relax the rules. Natasha was playing in the courtyard when her mother called her to supper. Natasha did not respond to the call, though she had obviously heard her mother.

"Natasha, I'm speaking to you. Come home immediately."

Natasha did not come in for another half hour. Glancing at her irritated mother she explained:

"We were playing boat. I couldn't jump out of the boat in the middle of the sea."

"And why didn't you answer?" the mother said, a little less angry.

"A storm was raging. You wouldn't have heard me," Natasha said.

The ability of the child to compare his actions with the demands of the adult, the Soviets call self-control, and self-control is the goal. With self-control, the child is able not only to hear what the adult says but to listen. Listening demands an inner connection between the child's consciousness and his actions, and when the child has gained this control of himself he does not need to be constantly reminded of the fact that he must listen attentively. Even a five-year-old will say, "Show me again; I wasn't listening," showing a realization of the necessity of this inner connection.

After they graduate from pedagogical college, kindergarten

teachers are expected constantly to improve their qualifications for teaching, with courses and seminars. The authorities complain that the same teachers take the courses year after year, while other teachers regularly avoid them.

There are periodic teachers' conferences. The minister of education, speaking to a conference of teachers in Moscow in April 1968, asked a question of vital interest to the Soviet state. He commented on the fact that children in play often took the parts of cosmonauts, flyers or sailors, but that no one ever wanted to play the part of a metalworker, carpenter or steelworker. "Why," he asked, "aren't these prosaic professions interesting to children?" This is definitely a problem today. Everyone wants to be an intellectual, and no one wants to be a worker.

·XIV·

Some Differences

JUST BEFORE OUR trip to the Soviet Union in the spring of 1969, my husband came home with a newspaper clipping his brother had sent us. He looked glum.

"They are going to abandon the whole preschool system in the Soviet Union," my husband said, handing me a clipping from the Los Angeles *Times*. I took it with cold, shaking hands, knowing that "they" *could* do such a thing, suddenly, unpredictably. The Central Committee of the Communist Party had taken sudden shifts in the past, making fools of some American experts on Soviet affairs. Any normally imaginative writer on Russian policies is haunted by a fear that by the time his words appear in print, they will be out of date. I read through the article.

It said that an unnamed Baltic demographer had suggested that Soviet kindergartens be closed and working mothers be allowed to remain at home to raise their children.

The article continued, saying that an even more telling attack on kindergartens had been made by Ekaterina Sheremeteva in an article in *Komsomolskaya Pravda*. Children brought up in kindergartens, Sheremeteva said, lag physically and mentally behind children brought up at home.

There was more, but I barely glanced over it on my way to the Congressional Library. At the library I could find no trace of the Baltic demographer mentioned in the article, but it did not take long to find the proper *Komsomolskaya Pravda*. The article was in the November 15, 1968, issue, and it was called "Kogda Skladyvaetsya Kharakter [When Character Is Formed]," by E. Sheremeteva, writer.

The article began with the statement that Ushinsky, Tolstoy, Bekhterev and Makarenko had agreed that the fundamentals of a personality were formed in early childhood and that much of the trouble with older children had its beginnings in the child's early years. "If you believe this," the article said, "it means that the parents, from the day of the child's birth, must take all the responsibility for him and not shift the responsibility to the state or to the grandmother."

Sheremeteva then quoted M. Koltsova, of the Pavlov Institute of Physiology: "In the development of the large hemisphere of the brain (that is, all the emotions and abilities) the greatest activity, most stormy in tempo, most grandiose in scale, takes place before the age of three." She added that the emotions could be trained like any other function of the nervous system, but that it was important that the child be treated with affection in his early years, or even his ability to love could be irreparably damaged.

From this, Sheremeteva concluded that the child should have individual attention at home in his first few years, instead of being taken to *yasli* at the age of five or six months. She described what she considered a typical scene:

The mother, with her baby in her arms, hurries to the *yasli*. She is lucky if she does not have to go on a crowded streetcar where the baby is jostled about, but at the *yasli* she thrusts the crying baby into a nurse's arms and goes off to her job, in tears herself. The baby, torn between home and *yasli,* is done serious harm. He has colds, and is otherwise physically ill. He needs individual attention at this age, not the divided attention of a *yasli* nurse who has fifteen or twenty children to look after.

To forestall criticism, Sheremeteva says she is not against collectivization, but that according to Professor Koltsova, it is only from the age of three that the child can benefit from the collectivization of a school, and that until the age of three the child is better off at home. Perhaps, she says, the mother's working day might be shortened during the time when she has children under three at home. In Hungary, she says, it was found that, for every child in *yasli,* 1.15 people were in the *yasli* personnel; so it was actually economically feasible for the mothers to stay at home.

Sheremeteva ended her article by saying that she was not a specialist herself and that the problem would be settled by the psychologists, pedagogists, sociologists, medical specialists and economists.

I was relieved to note several things not brought out in the Los Angeles *Times* article: The Soviet article said *yasli,* not kindergarten, and the main source quoted was a writer, not an educator. I was grateful to the *Times* for giving me the lead, and I set out looking for more articles.

Random items do not appear in Soviet newspapers. A controversial topic is launched, letters to the editor are read, and conclusions are reached. There is some freedom of the press, but it can easily be reined in when necessary. I did not have to wait long. *Komsomolskaya Pravda* for December 20, 1968, continued the argument.

Out of many letters on the subject, *Komsomolskaya Pravda* chose two. The first writer, a mother, agreed with the Sheremeteva article "from the first to the last line." Ninety percent of the mothers would agree, this mother said, that children should not go to *yasli* before the age of three. She stayed at home with her first son until he was a year old, she wrote, then since they needed the money, she got a job and tried to enroll her child in *yasli.* The *yasli* could not take him, so she and her husband took turns staying with the child, while both worked. In another year she tried the *yasli* again and this time the child was accepted.

"I shall never forget that day," she said. "My husband and I took Serozha to the group. He cried, and never stopped until three o'clock in the afternoon, when I went for him. These *yaslis,* I have to say, are very good, but his tears were without end."

Serozha's first day in kindergarten, she said, was entirely different. He liked it and told them at home about the fun he had had. Her second child started in *yasli* at the age of eight months and was sick so much that she missed a great deal of time from her job.

The second mother said that she thought the *yasli* was good but could be better. Her children were in the five-day group at *yasli,* and she said she didn't know what she would do without it. She worked during the day as an economist, and in the evening studied at the Marx-Lenin University. She liked to visit the Tretyakov Gallery and do other things she wouldn't be able to do if she had to sit at home with her two children. Both of her children liked *yasli,* she said. Both were normally developed emotionally, and both had dry noses. They got good care and good food in the *yasli.* She couldn't afford to feed them at home for the twelve rubles she paid the *yasli.* There were some problems she said—the parents might help more in the school work; the *yasli* could use a piano; some other improvements could be made.

At the proper moment, like the fishing guide who sits watching a fish run with his client's line, until it is time for professional help in landing the fish, Dr. Zaporozhets stepped into the argument with an article in *Pravda* on January 8, 1969, called "Detstvo: Semya i Yasli [Childhood: Family and Yasli]."

Dr. Zaporozhets said that the Preschool Institute had conducted a survey in twenty-five *yasli sads* in Moscow, Minsk, Kalinin, Rostov on the Don, Cherkass, and Zolotonosh. The results showed that children who attended *yasli* were more independent, more active, and better organized. They slept better, ate better, and were more oriented to everyday life than home raised children.

The writers complaining of *yasli* were apt to forget, he said, that most mothers worked, and the choice was not between *yasli* and mother but between *yasli* and grandmother, neighbor, older child or baby-sitter. Even if the mother stayed at home with the child, her attention was diverted by housework and other cares. In the family the child did not have the benefit of the collective, which was so important to *yasli.* In any event, he added, the *yasli* did not intend to replace the family but to educate the child in cooperation *with* the family.

Dr. Zaporozhets did not claim that the preschool system was perfect. Young children do have many colds, but steps are being taken to improve the situation. He seemed to think the *yasli* was particularly beneficial for children from a year and older.

In Russia, again, I asked the first kindergarten director we met what she thought of the argument. She did not know there had been an argument! She had not read any of the articles in *Pravda* and *Komsomolskaya Pravda*. I began to ask parents, guides, taxi drivers, and teachers about the articles. I even asked grandmothers sitting on park benches as they watched their grandchildren. Nobody had heard of the argument. No one had read any of the articles. I felt like saying, "You really should read *Pravda*. It has such interesting articles in it."

Although they had not read the articles, no one I asked failed to express an opinion. A Moscow taxi driver had sent his child to *yasli* when he was two months old, and he was pleased with the results. A Turkmenian taxi driver had five children, none of whom had been to *yasli* or kindergarten. His wife, who did not work, was perfectly capable of taking care of the children.

Some parents we asked, simply said, "We have Babushka," or even, "We have two grandmothers"—in full explanation of a child who did not go to *yasli*. When we asked a guide in Leningrad he said, "I'm not married." He seemed intrigued by the idea, however, and later said, "I'd send them to *yasli*."

"What about Babushka?" I asked.

"Oh," he said, "I forgot about her. I guess she'd want the children."

The teachers and directors of *kombinat*s, *yasli*s and *detsky sad*s felt there was no argument at all. Eventually all the children would go to *yasli*, where specialists could aid the family in raising the children. Mothers and grandmothers were not specialists. The only doubt we found expressed by the pedagogical side was from a methodist who said, "We have a saying, 'better a bad mother than a good teacher to the age of three. After that, a good teacher.' "

It was only at the Preschool Institute that I got the reaction I had expected. I had just started to say, "Have you read 'Kogda Skla—' " when everyone's eyes started flashing in instant reaction.

Everyone at the Institute had read every article, though they seemed more amused than alarmed by the controversy.

"Sheremeteva is a writer, not an educator," they said about the first article, the one which was quoted in the Los Angeles *Times*.

"Dr. Zaporozhets knows best," another said; and still another added, "Our main concern is continued improvement of pre-school institutions, not abandonment of them."

We did find that most of the people who disapproved of *yaslis* had never seen one. Several Intourist guides who went with us to preschool institutions seemd genuinely surprised at their high quality, and when I bought educational books in Soviet book-stores, I often found the guide asking for the same book a few minutes later.

I liked the *yasli* and *detsky sad* too. We saw a few runny noses, but most of the children seemed completely happy, and there were no prolonged tears. The relationship of *yasli* to child was anything but cold and institutional.

With the totality of control available to the Soviet state, there should be no distracting influences in attaining the goal set for education and yet the very totality of control itself constitutes a hazard. A concomitant of the totalitarian state is bureaucracy, which can be a very real threat to efficiency. In a five-month period the Leningorsk Polymetals Combine was "checked" by twenty commissions, causing Comrade Bulbis, the chief of the technical department, to exclaim in exasperation, "To hell with all these commissions."

Since nursery-kindergartens are built in conjunction with com-bines and factories, the red tape of building the kindergartens is added to the red tape of the plants. In new towns there must be seventy to ninety places in nursery-kindergartens for every thousand of the population. Thirty to thirty-five percent of these places are for children under three, and sixty-five to sev-enty percent for children between the ages of three and seven.

Athough school buildings are supposed to be built from standard plans, there are complaints that rural schools are often built from obsolete designs or by the local areas "on their own" and that these designs produce schools that are inferior to city schools. Once built, there are often troubles with repairs. In an article called "Ivan Passes the Buck to Peter," in *Pravda,* the troubles of one kindergarten were detailed.

At the beginning of March the kindergarten was closed for repairs, which the authorities said would take no more than a month and a half. At the end of the month not one nail had been hammered. Kravchenko, the writer who was complaining, said he was told not to worry, everything in the school was ready for the repairs. After three months of red tape, in which time Kravchenko was again told the matter was being investigated, he decided to write to *Pravda* for help. *Pravda* immediately sent a man to investigate.

"The kindergarten again!" said the manager of the trust, "What people!"

The *Pravda* investigator found that almost everyone was to blame. The workers of the trust, in their haste to close the kindergarten, had not prepared for its repairs. There were no building materials, no sanitary-technical equipment, no firm understanding with the contractors. The leaders of the trust passed the blame from one to another. The *Pravda* article ended with a threat and a hope: "We dare say that the *Gorkom* [town committee] will pay attention to this unattractive history."

The Soviet state is also concerned with family attitudes. Children enter first grade with varying levels of physical, mental and psychological preparation. One of the psychological problems involves children who have no fathers, either through divorce or the absence of marriage in the first place. In families in which both husband and wife work and they live in a crowded apartment, usually with a grandmother too, there are special stresses and strains. One Russian friend told us, showing some personal rancor, "Don't forget, every grandmother is also a mother-in-law"—a fact which is irritatingly apparent to many a Russian.

Theoretically there should be no unwanted children, since abortions are both legal and free, provided they are performed in a hospital by a competent doctor. In practice, since the state has a liberal view of illegitimacy, and since, because of war deaths, there were more women than men, there are many children without fathers. According to a 1944 law, a man who had not registered marriage with the mother of his child bore no parental obligation.

The 1944 decree caused a storm of argument and protest. The Soviet magazine *Nedeliya* (*The Week*) claimed that since 1944 there had been "several million miracles of virgin birth—the father, like the Holy Spirit, is indicated by a blank space in the birth certificate."

In 1954 the magazine *Literaturnaya Gazeta* (*Literary Newspaper*) launched a campaign against the 1944 law. Writers, scientists, public figures, jurists and ordinary readers joined in the discussions. A teacher was interested in what the illegitimate child should be called—" 'Illegitimate,' 'illicit,' or in the French manner, 'bastard'?" She wrote that she had taught fifteen hundred children, three hundred of whom had a blank space on their birth certificate after the word, "father."

"It is not enough that the child grows up without a father. Why should he also suffer affront, insult, shame, seeing his documents differ from those of others? Ten- and twelve-year-old children shout at their classmates: 'Hey, you fatherless!' "

In 1968, a law was passed with a clause which still did not satisfy everyone, but no longer left a blank space on the illegitimate child's record. According to the new law, if the parents are unmarried, the name of the child's mother is recorded on the application by the mother, and the name of the child's father is recorded on joint application of the child's father and mother, or the father's name is recorded in accordance with the decision of the court.

If neither joint parental application nor court decision has been made to establish paternity, the surname of the father is recorded in the birth records under the mother's surname. The name and patronymic of the child's father are recorded as the mother instructs.

Despite this controversy, there is no talk of a disadvantaged child, as there is in the United States. The child himself seldom feels that his state does not care about him, whether he has a father or not. The unmarried mother gets a substantial reduction in *yasli* and *detsky sad* fees for her child, but he goes to the same school the children with fathers go to, even when the fathers are affluent.

Because of the reduction in the primary grades in the Soviet Union from four to three years, the preschools now must more carefully prepare their children for school. (The problem of what to do with the children who have not attended kindergarten has been solved in Moscow by requiring special make-up classes, but kindergarten attendance is far from universal in other parts of the Soviet Union.)

The 1969 *Program* has perfected the 1965 *Program,* on which an American translation was based. More stress is put on learning, specifically reading and writing, and more independent activity is encouraged.

One of the most startling changes is that the three-year-olds, who in activities like drawing had not been divided into subgroups before, are now being put into small groups with the same level of development. Previously, the Soviets had not approved of dividing children according to ability.

The new program also puts more stress on the physical well-being of the children, particularly the *yasli* children. The theme of the new program is better orientation to the child's surroundings, with special stress laid on creating a rhythm of life which carries through the entire educational system.

The Soviet child may expect to have a better life than his father had, just as his father has more than *his* father had; but the way to that better life is through education, and he does not need to be reminded of Lenin's admonition to "study, study, study." The Soviet commitment to education is as great as its commitment to Communism.

·APPENDIX·

Sample work schedules

Appendix

Schedule for Children of Three Months to One Year

At Home:	3–6 months	6–10 months	10 months–1 year
—Wake up, feeding, get up	6–7:00	6–7:00	
—Wake up, get up			6:30–7:00
At Kindergarten:			
—Arrival, inspection, undressing, play in crib or on floor	7–8:00	7–8:00	7–8:00
—Lie down, sleep in fresh air	7:30–9:30	8–10:00	
—Breakfast			7:30–8:30
—Play, activity			8:30–9:00
—Lie down, sleep in fresh air			9:00–11:30
—Get up, feeding	9:30–10:00	10–10:45	
—Get up, dinner			11:30–12:30
—Play, activity	10–11:00	10:45–12:00	12:30–14:30
—Sleep in fresh air	11–13:00	12–14:00	14:30–16:00
—Get up, feeding	13–13:30	14–14:45	
—Get up, *poldnik*			16–17:00
—Get up, play, activity	13:30–14:30	14:45–16	17–18:00
—Lie down, sleep in fresh air	14:30–16:30	16–18:00	
—Get up, feeding	16:30–17:30	18–18:30	
—Parents take children	17:00	18:00	18:00
At Home:			
—Sleep	18–19:30		
—Bathing, feeding	19:30–20:30		
—Bathing, lie down		19:30–20:00	
—Play, walk			18–19:00
—Bath, supper			19–19:30
—Sleep	20:30–6:00	20:00–6:00	20–6:30
—Feeding	23:30	22:00	23:00

SCHEDULE FOR THE TWO-TO-THREE-YEAR-OLDS

AT HOME:	
Get up, morning toilet	6:30–7:30
IN THE KINDERGARTEN:	
Arrival of children, inspection, play	7:00–8:00
Preparation for breakfast, breakfast	7:50–8:35
Play in subgroups	8:35–9:30
Preparation for walk, walk	9:15–11:15
Return from walk, undressing, play	11:15–11:40
Preparation for dinner, dinner	11:40–12:30
Preparation for nap, nap in open air	12:30–15:30
Awakening from nap, air-water procedure, play	15:30–16:00
Preparation for *poldnik, poldnik*	16:00–16:30
Play, activity	16:30–17:00
Play, go home	17:00–19:00
AT HOME:	
Play	till 19:20
Preparation for supper, supper	19:20–20:15
Preparation for bed	20:15–20:30
Sleep	20:30–6:30, 7:00

Schedule for the Three-to-Four-Year-Olds

Fall and Winter Period:

At Home:	
Get up, morning toilet	6:30–7:30

In the Kindergarten:	
Arrival of children, inspection, play	7:00–8:00
Preparation for breakfast, breakfast	8:00–8:45
Play, preparation for activities	8:45–9:15
Activities	9:15–9:30
Preparation for walk, walk	9:30–12:00
Preparation for dinner, dinner	12:00–12:45
Preparation for sleep, sleep	12:45–15:00
Awaken from nap, air-water procedure, play	15:00–16:00
Preparation for *poldnik, poldnik*	16:00–16:30
Preparation for walk, walk, go home	16:30–19:00

At Home:	
Play	19:00–19:30
Preparation for supper, supper	19:30–20:00
Peaceful play, preparation for bed	20:00–20:30
Sleep	20:30–6:30, 7:00

In January and February, regular gymnastics in the morning. In summer, one activity: music, nature watching, or watching work of people, reading and stories.

SCHEDULE FOR THE FOUR-TO-FIVE-YEAR-OLDS

AT HOME:
Get up, morning toilet	6:30–7:30

IN KINDERGARTEN:
Arrival of children, inspection, play, on duty, morning gymnastics	7:00–8:20
Preparation for breakfast, breakfast	8:20–9:00
Play, preparation for activities	9:00–9:30
Activities	9:30–10:00
Preparation for walk, walk	10:00–12:15
Preparation for dinner, dinner	12:15–13:00
Preparation for nap, nap	13:00–15:00
Get up, air-water procedure, play	15:00–16:00
Preparation for *poldnik, poldnik*	16:00–16:15
Play, preparation for walk, walk, go home	16:15–19:00

AT HOME:
Play	19:00–19:30
Preparation for supper, supper	19:30–19:50
Quiet play, preparation for bed	19:50–20:45
Sleep	20:45–6:30, 7:00

·BIBLIOGRAPHY·

ENGLISH-LANGUAGE SOURCES:

Almy, Millie C., *Young Children's Thinking*, New York: Teacher's College Press, 1966.

Beauty as the Mainspring of Education. Moscow: Novosti Press Agency Publishing House, n.d.

Bryce, Mayo, *Fine Arts Education in the Soviet Union*. Washington, D.C.: U.S. Government Printing Office, 1963.

Current Digest of the Soviet Press, The. A weekly digest of Russian sources translated into English; a valuable and fascinating source of information on Soviet life, it should be read by everyone. Published by the American Association for the Advancement of Slavic Studies, Ohio State University, Columbus, Ohio.

Current Soviet Policies, IV. New York: Columbia University Press, 1962.

Deineko, M., *Public Education in the U.S.S.R.* Moscow: Progress Publishers, n.d.

Documentary and Reference Material on Education in the Soviet Union, Alexander G. Korol, ed. Cambridge, Mass.: Center for International Studies, Massachusetts Institute of Technology, 1956.

Educational Psychology in the U.S.S.R., Brian and Joan Simon, eds. Stanford, Calif.: Stanford University Press, 1963.

Education in the U.S.S.R., Fred Ablin, ed., 2 vols. White Plains, N.Y.: International Arts and Sciences Press, 1963.

Krupskaya, Nadezhda K., *On Education*. Moscow: Foreign Languages Publishing House, 1957.

Luria, A. R., *The Role of Speech in the Regulation of Normal and Abnormal Behavior*. New York: Pergamon Press, 1961.

Makarenko, Anton Semyonovich, *A Book for Parents*. Moscow: Foreign Languages Publishing House, n.d.

———, *Learning to Live*. Moscow: Foreign Languages Publishing House, 1953.

———, *Problems of Soviet School Education*. Moscow: Progress Publishers, 1965.

——, *The Road to Life,* trans. by Ivy and Tatiana Litvinov. Moscow: Foreign Languages Publishing House, n.d.

Moscow News. An English-language weekly newspaper published in Moscow.

O'Connor, N., *Recent Soviet Psychology.* New York: Pergamon Press, 1961.

Piaget, Jean, *The Language and Thought of the Child.* New York: Meridian Books, 1955.

Present Day Russian Psychology, Neil O'Connor, ed. London: The Commonwealth and International Library. Pergamon Press, 1966.

Simon, Brian, *Psychology in the Soviet Union.* London: Routledge and Kegan Paul, 1957.

Sokolov, Ye. N., *Perception and the Conditioned Reflex.* New York: Pergamon Press, 1943.

Soviet Education, George L. Kline, ed. London: Routledge and Kegan Paul, 1957.

Soviet Education. Periodical containing translations of Soviet educational articles; as indispensable as *The Current Digest of the Soviet Press.* Published by the International Arts and Sciences Press, White Plains, N.Y.

Soviet Educators on Soviet Education, Helen B. Redl, ed. and trans. London: Free Press of Glencoe-Collier Macmillan, 1964.

Soviet Preschool Education: Vol. I, *Program of Instruction;* Vol. II, *Teacher's Commentary.* New York: Holt, Rinehart and Winston, 1969. Translation of the 1965 *Program.*

Soviet Psychology and Psychiatry. Magazine published by International Arts and Sciences Press, 108 Grand Street, White Plains, N.Y.

Sputnik. English-language periodical published in Moscow.

U.S.S.R., Questions and Answers. Moscow: Novosti Press Agency Publishing House, n.d.

Vygotsky, Lev Semyonovich, *Thought and Language.* Cambridge, Mass.: Massachusetts Institute of Technology Press, 1962.

RUSSIAN-LANGUAGE SOURCES:

Babadzhan, T. S., *Muzykalnoye Vospitanie Detei Rannego Vozrasta.* Moscow: Izdatelstvo Prosveshchenie, 1967.

Beltyukov, V. I., *Chtenie s Gub Foneticheskikh Elementov Rechi.* Moscow: Izdatelstvo Prosveshchenie, 1967.

Berzina, A. K., *Geograficheskie Igry v Shkole.* Moscow: Izdatelstvo Prosveshchenie, 1966.

Deti s Otkloneniyami v Razvitii, M. S. Pevzner, ed. Moscow: Izdatelstvo Prosveshchenie, 1966.

BIBLIOGRAPHY

Didakticheskie Igry i Zanyatiya, E. I. Radina, ed. Moscow: Izdatelstvo Prosveshchenie, 1967.

Dmitrieva, N. A., *Voprosy Esteticheskogo Vospitaniya*. Moscow: Gosizdat Iskusstvo, 1956.

Dobreitser, V., *Meditsinskoye Obsluzhivanie Detei v Doshkolnykh Uchrezhdeniya*. Moscow: Izdatelstvo Prosveshchenie, 1967.

Doshkolnoye Vospitanie (magazine).

Dyakonova, T. G., and Shcherbak, M. K., *Albbom*. Moscow: Izdatelstvo Prosveshchenie, 1966.

Elkonin, D. B. *Detskaya Psikhologiya*. Moscow: Uchpedgiz, 1960.

Fomichev, A. P., N. K. *Krupskaya, Ob Esteticheskom Vospitanii*. Moscow: Izdatelstvo A.P.N., R.S.F.S.R., 1963.

Frenkel, Nina, *Stikhi i Pesni Detyam*. Minsk: Izdatelstvo Narodnaya Asveta, 1966.

Gorodilova, V. I., and Kuzmina, N. I., *Vospitanie Rechi Detei Logonevrotikov*. Moscow: Uchpedgiz, 1960.

Gorodilova, V. I., and Radina, E. I., *Vospitanie Pravelnoi Rechi u Detei Doshkolnogo Vozrasta*. Moscow: Uchpedgiz, 1961.

Grineva, Natalya, *Malenkie Grazhdane*. Moscow: Izdatelstvo Prosveshchenie, 1967.

Igra i Trud v. Detskom Sadu, A. P. Usova and L. A. Penevska, eds. Moscow: Izdatelstvo A.P.N., R.S.F.S.R., 1961.

Iova, E., *Programma Prazdnika v Detskom Sadu*. Leningrad: Izdatelstvo Muzyka, 1967.

Istoriya Pedagogiki, N. A. Konstantinov, E. N. Medinskii and M. F. Shabaeva, eds. Moscow: Izdatelstvo Prosveshchenie, 1966.

Izvestia (daily newspaper).

Kilpio, N. N., *80 Igr Vospitalelyu Detskovo Sada*. Moscow: Izdatelstov Prosveshchenie, 1965.

Koltsova, M. M., *Vospitanie Polesnykh Navykov i Privychek u Detei*. Moscow: Izdatelstvo Meditsina, 1965.

Komsomolskaya Pravda (periodical).

Krasnogorskaya, L. I., *Rol Semi v Vospitanii Doshkolnika*. Moscow: Uchpedgiz, 1959.

Krokodil (periodical).

Krupskaya, N. K., *Izbrannye Pedagogicheskie Proisvedeniya*. Moscow: Izdatelstvo A.P.N., R.S.F.S.R., 1955.

Krylova, E. T., *Vospitanie Malenkogo Rebenka v Seme*. Moscow: Medgiz, 1959.

Leninskii Sbornik, Pismo I. V. Stalinu, Vol. 36 (Moscow, 1933), p. 515.

Leontev, A. N., *Oshchushcheniya, Vospriyatiya i Vnimanie Detei Mladshego Shkolnogo Vozrasta*. Moscow: Izdatelstvo A.P.N., R.S.F.S.R., 1950.

Leushina, A. M., *Obuchenie Schyoty v Detskom Sadu*. Moscow: Uchpedgiz, 1961.

BIBLIOGRAPHY

Levitov, N. D., *Detskaya i Pedagogicheskaya Psikhologiya*. Moscow: Gos-ucheb-ped Izdatelstvo Ministerstva Prosveshcheniya R.S.F.S.R., 1960.

Levshin, L. A., *Daite Pedagogicheskii Sovyet*. Moscow: Izdatelstvo Politicheskoi Literatury, 1965.

Lichnost i Trud, K. K. Plamonov, ed. Moscow: Izdatelstvo Mysl, 1965.

Lishtvan, E. V., *Igry i Zanyatiya so Stroitelnym Materialom v Detskom Sadu*. Moscow: Izdatelstvo Prosveshchenie, 1967.

Literaturnaya Gazeta (periodical).

Lomova, T. P., *Muzykalnye Kartinki*. Moscow: Izdatelstvo Prosveshchenie, 1966.

Luria, A. R., and Yudovich, D. Ya., *Rech i Razvitie Psikhicheskikh Protsessov u Rebenka*. Moscow: Izdatelstvo A.P.N., R.S.F.S.R., 1957.

Lyublinskaya, A. A., *Ocherki Psikhicheskogo Razvitiya Rebenka*. Moscow: Izdatelstvo A.P.N., R.S.F.S.R., 1959.

Mekhanizmy Recheobrazovaniya i Vospriyatiya Slozhnykh Zvukov. Moscow, Leningrad: Izdatelstvo Nauka, 1966.

Merzhan, Ida, *Lyubish-li Ty Menya, Mama?* Moscow: Izdatelstvo Prosveshchenie, 1968.

Mikhailova, L. E., and Metlov, N. A., *Prazdnichnye Utrenniki v Detskom Sadu*. Moscow: Izdatelstvo Muzyka, 1967.

Murzilka (periodical).

Myasnigov, A. P., *O Vospitanii Detei*. Leningrad: Gosizdat Meditsinskoi Literatury, 1959.

Narodnoye Obrazovanie v S.S.S.R. Moscow: Izdatelstvo Prosveshchenie, 1967.

Narushenie Rechi u Doshkolnikov. Moscow: Izdatelstvo Prosveshchenie, 1969.

Nauki i Religiya (periodical).

Nauki i Zhizn (periodical).

Nechaeva, V. G., Markova, T. A., Zhukovskaya, P. I., and Penevskaya, L. A., *Formirovanie Kollektivnykh Vzaimootnoshenii Detei Starshego Vozrasta*. Moscow: Izdatelstvo Prosveshchenie, 1968.

Novaya Vremya (periodical).

Novy Mir (periodical).

Osakina, Tatiana I., *Podvizhnye Igry Dlya Malyshei*. Moscow: Izdatelstvo Prosveshchenie, 1965.

Osnovy Politicheskikh Znanii. Moscow: Gosizdat Politicheskoi Literatury, 1962.

Ot Nolya do Semi. Moscow: Izdatelstvo Znanie, 1967.

Podgotovka Detei v Detskom Sadu k Shkole, A. P. Usova, ed. Moscow: Izdatelstvo A.P.N., R.S.F.S.R., 1955.

Popova, M. M., "Nachalo Rechevogo Obshcheniya u Detei Rannego Vozrasta," *Umstvennoye Vospitanie Detei Rannego Vozrasta*, E. I.

Radina, ed. Moscow: Izdatelstvo Prosveshchenie, 1968.

Pravda (daily newspaper).

Problemy Obucheniya i Vospitaniya v Nachalnoi Shkole, B. G. Ananev and A. I. Sorokina, eds. Moscow: Uchepedgiz, 1960.

Programma Vospitaniya v Detskom Sadu. Moscow: Uchpedgiz, 1962, 1965.

Razvitie i Vospitanie Detei Rannego Vozrasta, N. M. Aksarina, ed. Leningradskoye Otdelenie: Izdatelstvo Meditsina, 1965.

Razvitie Vospriyatiya v Rannem i Doshkolnom Detstve, A. V. Zaporozhets and M. I. Lisina, eds. Moscow: Izdatelstvo Prosveshchenie, 1966.

Roditeli i Deti, E. I. Volkova, ed. Moscow: Izdatelstvo A.P.N., R.S.F.S.R., 1961.

Rol Igry v Detskom Sadu, A. P. Usova, ed. Izdatelstvo A.P.N., R.S.F.S.R., 1961.

Rozhdestvenskaya, V. I., and Pavlova, A. I., *Podvizhnye Igry Dlya Zaikayushchegosya Doshkolnika.* Moscow: Izdatelstvo Prosveshchenie, 1967.

Rudneva, E. I., *Pedagogicheskaya Sistema N. K. Krupskoi.* Moscow: Izdatelstvo Moskovskogo Universiteta, 1968.

Samye Malenkie v Detskom Sadu, compiled by N. Ya. Ivanova and E. A. Lebedeva. Moscow: Izdatelstvo Prosveshchenie, 1967.

Sbornik po Slushaniyu Muzyki, compiled by I. N. Sak. Minsk: Izadetelstvo Narodnaya Asveta, 1965.

Semya i Shkola (periodical).

Sensornoye Vospitanie Doshkolnikov, A. V. Zaporozhets and A. P. Usova, eds. Moscow: Izdatelstvo A.P.N., R. S.F.S.R., 1963.

Shif, Zh. I., *Usvoenie Yazyka i Razvitie Myshleniya u Glukhikh Detei.* Moscow: Izdatelstvo Prosveshchenie, 1968.

Shkola, Detskii Sad i Semya, E. I. Volkova, ed. Moscow: Izdatelstvo A.P.N., R.S.F.S.R., 1959.

Shkola, Semya i Obshchestvennost, E. I. Volkova, ed. Moscow: Izdatelstvo A.P.N., R.S.F.S.R., 1963.

Sorokina, A., *Didakticheskie Igry v Detskom Sadu.* Moscow: Gos-uchebno-pedagog Izdatelstvo, 1955.

Sostoyanie Obucheniya v Detskikh Sadakh, A. P. Usova, ed. Moscow: Izdatelstvo A.P.N., R.S.F.S.R., 1960.

Sovyetskaya Pedagogika (periodical).

Spravochnik po Doshkolnomu Vospitaniyu, compiled by A. I. Zorina-Tarasova. Moscow: Izdatelstvo Prosveshchenie, 1967.

Studenikin, M. Ya., Novikova, E. Ya., Dombrovskaya, M. P., and Krylova, E. G., *Ukhod Vskarmlivanie i Vospitanie Rebenka Pervogo Goda Zhinzni.* Moscow: Izdatelstvo Meditsina, 1966.

Svadkovskii, I. F., *O Vospitanii Trudolyubiya u Detei.* Moscow: Uchpedgiz, 1959.

Bibliography

Tikheyeva, E. I., *Igry i Zanyatiya Malykh Detei*. Moscow: Izdatelstvo Prosveshchenie, 1965.

———, *Razvitie Rechi Detei*. Moscow: Izdatelstvo Prosveshchenie, 1967.

Trud i Nablyudeniya v Prirode, compiled by A. F. Mazurina. Moscow: Izdatelstvo Prosveshchenie, 1967.

Trudovoye Vospitanie v Detskom Sadu. V. G. Nechaeva, ed. Moscow: Izdatelstvo Prosveshchenie, 1964.

Uchitelskaya Gazeta (newspaper).

Usova, A. P., *Detskii Sad*. Moscow: Izdatelstvo A.P.N., R.S.F.S.R., 1951.

———, *Zanyatiya v Detskom Sadu po Russkomu Yazyku*. Moscow: Gosuchebno Pedagog Izdatelstvo, 1954.

Uznadze, D. N., *Psikhologicheskie Issledovaniya*. Moscow: Izdatelstvo Nauka, 1966.

Vasilkov, G. A., *Gimnastika*. Moscow: Izdatelstvo Prosveshchenie, 1966.

Veselye Kartinki (periodical).

Vetlugina, N. A., *Metody Obucheniya Peniyu Detei Doshkolnogo Vozrasta*. Moscow: Izdatelstvo A.P.N., R.S.F.S.R., 1955.

———, *Muzykalnoye Razvitie Rebenka*. Moscow: Izdatelstvo Prosveshchenie, 1968.

———, *Muzykalnye Zanyatiya v Detskom Sadu*. Moscow: Uchpedgiz, 1958.

———, *Muzykalnyi Bukvar*. Moscow: Muzgiz, 1961.

———, *Muzyka v Detskom Sadu*. Moscow: Izdatelstvo Muzyka, 1965.

———, *Oktyabr*. Moscow: Izdatelstvo Muzyka, 1967.

———, *Sistema Esteticheskogo Vospitaniya v Detskom Sadu*. Moscow: Izdatelstvo A.P.N., R.S.F.S.R., 1962.

———, *Vyshli Deti v Sadik*. Moscow: Izdatelstvo Muzyka, 1966.

Voprosy Pedagogiki Rannego Detstva, N. M. Aksarina and E. I. Radina, eds. Moscow: Izdatelstvo Prosveshchenie, 1964.

Voskresenskaya, A. I., *Gramota v Detskom Sadu*. Moscow: Izdatelstvo Prosveshchenie, 1965.

Vospitanie Detei Tretego Goda Zhizni v Doshkolnom Uchrezhdenii, V. G. Nechaeva, ed. Moscow: Izdatelstvo Prosveshchenie, 1965.

Vospitanie i Obuchenie Detei s Rasstroistvami Rechi, S. S. Lyapidevskii and V. I. Seliverstova, eds. Moscow: Izdatelstvo Prosveshchenie, 1968.

Vospitanie i Obuchenie Slepogo Doshkolnika, L. N. Solntseva, ed. Moscow: Izdatelstvo Prosveshchenie, 1967.

Vospominaniya o N. K. Krupskoi, A. G. Kravchenko, ed. Moscow: Izdatelstvo Prosveshchenie, 1966.

Yakovlev, V., and Grinevskii, A., *Igry Dlya Detei*. Moscow: Izdatelstvo Fizkulturna i Sport, 1968.

Zaporozhets, A. V., *Psikhologiya*. Moscow: Gosudarstvennoye Uchebno

Bibliography

Pedagogicheskoye Izdatelstvo Ministerstva Prosveshcheniya, R.S.F.S.R., 1961.

———, *Razvitie Proisvolnykh Dvizhenii.* Moscow: Izdatelstvo A.P.N., R.S.F.S.R., 1960.

Zhukovskaya, P. I., *Vospitanie Rebenka v Igre.* Moscow: Izdatelstvo A.P.N., R.S.F.S.R., 1963.

·INDEX·

· INDEX ·

INDEX